PSYCHOLOGY OF PANDEMICS:

" A CENTURY WHERE PSYCHOLOGY HAS INFLUENCED THE SURVIVAL OF THE ECONOMY "

BOOK INTRODUCTION

This Book **"Psychology Of Pandemic"** Is a masterpiece and an in depth fundamental content that makes a deep and absolute evaluations, measures, explanation, process, facts, response, and all peripherals surrounding the circles of pandemic.

It is a multi- faceted piece, that also talks about our **psychological and mental feelings** towards an insecure situation, which is the **"pandemic"** , our fears, mental effects, anxiety, and all other variables that jeopardizes the situation, following tips and ethical considerations on what we can do to overcome our fears towards a pandemic uncertainty.

Of course, it's natural to experience stress, anxiety, grief, and worry during and after a stressful situation. No one reacts the same way, and your own feelings will change over time. Notice and accept how you feel. If you take care of your emotional health during an illness, it will help you think clearly and protect yourself and your family. Taking care of yourself during a stressful situation will help you in your long-term recovery.

Reactions during a pandemic include: Fears and worries about your health and that of your loved ones who may have been exposed to such disease, changes in sleep patterns or eating habits, difficulty sleeping or concentrating, the worsening of chronic health problems, increased use of alcohol, tobacco or other drugs, all

Every pandemic involves changes and dangers at the biological, psychological and social levels . Now we realize more clearly than ever. Until now, almost thirty centuries after the birth of scientific medicine, we thought, and with reason, that the dangers were primarily biological. And it is like this: the term pandemic must be circumscribed to its biological realities, that is, to the danger that it represents for the life and health of citizens, and the world at largeThat is why reducing the risk of infection was a clear survival advantage . For this reason, we evolve a set of unconscious psychological responses to act as a first line of defense to reduce our contact with potential pathogens.

No matter the circumstances that sorrounds the world at large, it is important for us to know that our mental health will be one way or the other affected emotional, which is as a result of fear, and different health related phobias and feelings. Then it is our duty to make sure that we timely and effectively control these emotional distress for us to be able to maintain a good hygiene and living at it's peak, as a result of finding a remedy to some of these psychological effects on our mental health because of pandemic situations, this book was ten birth to provide a thorough guidelines on how we can overcome these reactions efficiently and effectively without any hinderances at all cost.

Well, much cannot be said here as this is an intro, why can't you read on?.. the chapters are down below.

BEST REGARDS.

Table of contents

CHAPTER ONE

Throughout its history, humanity has experienced numerous diseases that have ended the lives of thousands of people. Surely you have heard about cholera or Ebola on television and you want to know the difference between pandemic and epidemic.

The spread of infectious diseases has been due to the emergence of risk factors such as poverty or poor hygiene caused by natural disasters or armed conflict. In these situations, diseases that pose a health hazard spread rapidly.

What is the meaning of pandemic?

According to the World Health Organization (WHO), the global spread of a new disease is called a pandemic . For example, a pandemic occurs the moment a new flu virus appears and spreads around the world because almost no one has any defenses against it.

Most of the pandemics have been caused by influenza viruses that affect animals. Surely you remember the famous bird flu.

There is talk of a pandemic when a disease of viral origin begins to spread rapidly throughout the world, affecting a very high number of people. The means to combat such a phenomenon are quite limited, so it is very important to prevent in order to act in time.

One of the characteristics that best defines a pandemic is the great ease with which the disease is spread and passes from one person to another. This high degree of contagion favors two things. The first is that the number of people infected with the virus in question is growing very rapidly, and the second is that the number of countries affected is growing equally rapidly.

What is an epidemic?

According to the SAR, an epidemic is a disease that spreads for some time through a country, simultaneously affecting large numbers of people.

Difference between pandemic and epidemic

However, the difference between pandemic and epidemic lies in two aspects:

- The expansion from the geographical point of view of the disease.
- The rapid increase in cases of people affected by the disease.

In a pandemic both aspects have greater proportions than in an epidemic. The level of health emergency caused by an epidemic and a pandemic depends on:

- How the disease spreads.
- The ease of propagation.
- The possibility of contagion from affected people to healthy ones.
- The relationship between people who are in danger of contagion and immune people (for having been vaccinated, for example).

In addition to pandemics and epidemics, we can also speak of endemics. According to the definition of the SAR, an endemic is a disease that usually reigns at fixed times in a country or region .

Therefore, these are cases of normal diseases that frequently affect a country or area depending on the season of the year. Although the disease affects many people, in general it is not serious cases.

Currently the existence of epidemics or pandemics can be detected by analyzing incidents in a certain area over a period of time.

Why does it spread so quickly?

As it is a virus of animal origin, most human beings lack the necessary defenses to combat it, which favors its rapid spread. Ironically, the people who are most in contact with the animal spice from which the virus has arisen are the most prepared to face the disease, since they have developed the necessary defenses to cope with it.

What can be done to fight a pandemic?

As it is a viral disease, it would take several months, at least, to develop a vaccine that could immunize people against the virus that causes the disease. Therefore, the best remedy is prevention. It is vitally important to locate the focus where a pandemic starts in time to implement a series of protocols to isolate the area and stop its expansion.

The WHO (World Health Organization), in an attempt to plan and organize the response to a possible pandemic outbreak, has established six levels of alert:

-Level 1: The existence of a potentially dangerous virus for human beings is verified, but it still circulates exclusively among animals.

-Level 2: There is a case of contagion of the virus from animals to people, but in isolation.

-Level 3: The virus begins to spread from person to person. Still, these are still isolated cases.

-Level 4: The transmission of the virus from person to person is generalized, leading to small outbreaks of considerable importance in certain regions of the world. When this level is reached, the risk of a global pandemic begins to be considerable.

-Level 5: The spread of the virus between human beings continues, being affected at this time by at least two countries in the same region. When this level is reached, the risk of a global pandemic becomes very high.

-Level 6: The full pandemic phase is reached. The virus spreads rapidly, affecting an increasing number of people in an increasing number of countries.

History has left us several pandemics, all of them affecting a vast number of people with diseases such as smallpox, diphtheria, tuberculosis or the flu.

-The black plague, which hit Europe in the mid-fourteenth century. This pandemic originated in Asia, and from there it reached Europe by crossing the Mediterranean. Black plague is estimated to have killed about 20 million people.

-Spanish flu. A pandemic whose origin was never found and which ended in the lives of some 25 million people in places as far apart as the United States, the United Kingdom and India.

-AIDS (acquired immunodeficiency syndrome). One of the great pandemics of the late 20th century, this disease experienced its period of maximum expansion in the 1980s. AIDS is a sexually transmitted disease and is estimated to have killed 20 to 25 million people worldwide.

Management And Control Of Uncertainty In An Emerging Influenza Pandemic

The early stages of an epidemic require decision-making with predictable challenges, an aspect that became evident with the current influenza A (H1N1) virus. The scale of the problem is uncertain when a disease first arises, but it can spread quickly. It is important that decisions are made when the threat is only modest, which implies an in-depth analysis of the socio-economic consequences that an energetic vaccination program, the school and work holidays can have in the face of an epidemic that is only in its early stage .

Mild reactions to a seasonal influenza-like strain are justified with a mortality of approximately 0.1% in infected patients, with higher rates among the very young and the elderly. When it comes to a pandemic with a death rate of 2% or more and affects middle-aged people, more vigorous action must be taken.

In the United States, for example, on May 4 the mark of 1000 cases passed and the second death was reported on May 5. Coldly speaking, the case-death rate would be 0.2%, just the upper limit of seasonal flu.

However, there are two main sources of uncertainty that substantially affect severity estimates. The proportion of severe cases is overestimated in situations where many minor cases are not reported or studied, a situation that becomes more frequent as health providers are unable to evaluate by laboratory studies a large fraction of suspected cases. In contrast, severity estimates suffer from underreporting when they are calculated as simple indexes of the number of deaths with the number of cases, because there is a delay between the onset of illness and death. Thanks to current treatments, this interval is currently much longer than in the 1918 flu pandemic.

There are also other factors that suggest not underestimating the severity of this pandemic. First, the virus tends to infect relatively young and healthy people and produces a high rate of hospitalizations (2%).

Second, the much higher proportion of people likely to become infected in a pandemic (due to limited immunity to the new strain) will mean substantially higher levels of unfavorable outcomes. A virus that has an assumed mortality of only 0.15%, but infects twice or more cases than seasonal flu, will cause three times more death than this. On the other hand, developing countries will have much higher mortality than developed countries.

The Northern Hemisphere can see a decline in transmission throughout the summer, but the 1918 pandemic showed that sustained transmission is possible during the spring and summer when a new strain of virus emerges. For its part, the Southern Hemisphere is entering the seasonal flu period and is at risk, along with the rest of the world, of a major pandemic for the coming months, with infection rates higher than seasonal flu, before being able to dispose of vaccines.

School absenteeism, a gross measure of the spread of the epidemic, will be worthless as schools close in the summer.

When a vaccine is available, due to its limited availability, knowledge of pre-existing immunity, the most affected age groups and other factors that depend on reliable determinations on the incidence of mild and severe cases of the disease will be necessary. .

If the infection remains mild in most cases, it can be considered similar to that of a regular seasonal epidemic. Unfortunately, pandemic viruses tend to mutate during the seasons and become more aggressive.

Serological surveys represent screenshots in the population rather than a real-time determination of incidence.

Surveillance of nonspecific indicators such as consultations and visits by health providers, as well as hospitalizations, can provide an indication of the total burden of the disease, but do not determine the cause. Therefore, this surveillance should be combined with routine studies of systematic samples of patients to assess the total burden of disease attributable to the H1N1 virus, its variations with age and other risk factors.

Detailed investigations of transmissions in homes and schools will clarify dynamic transmissions and generate recommendations and prevention measures.

Increasing traditional surveillance for the new virus should be a high priority. For example, daily school absenteeism, in real time, should be recorded, detecting the most affected age groups and other factors. Using cell phones to report survey results can be another method of real-time surveillance in resource-limited areas.

International collaboration is crucial, not only to increase surveillance capacity in the tropics and in the Southern Hemisphere, but also to control changes in antigenicity, gravity, transmissibility, and antiviral resistance that can be reflected in an autumn wave in the Northern Hemisphere. .

Many suggested approaches to improve the environmental awareness of the epidemic during its passage through the Northern Hemisphere can be applied more immediately in the tropics and in the Southern Hemisphere when the seasonal epidemic reaches that area.

Surveillance systems and acquired knowledge of the dynamics of infectious disease transmission have improved substantially since the 1968 flu pandemic and can be used as health guides in the current pandemic.

Conclusion

Public information about risk and uncertainty is essential. Conflicting statements and recommendations need to be avoided, and the extent of the pandemic must be reported objectively. Decisions must be made even if there is no definitive estimate of the severity of the pandemic. For example, the decision to produce a flu pandemic vaccine instead of the seasonal epidemic will have to be made in the next month.

Also, the United States will have to decide very soon the use of complementary vaccines to protect a greater number of people with a certain amount of antigen, although they are not currently licensed. As always, the main victims of delays in these decisions will be developing countries that will have less access to these vaccines and will suffer the greatest impact from the pandemic.

CHAPTER TWO:

PSYCHOLOGICAL EFFECTS OF PANDEMIC

Beyond the terrible effects on our health, the pandemic brings us psychological and social consequences. Fortunately, fear is not the only emotion that can rule us.

Everyone has been upset by the recent pandemic that befall the world, the coronavirus . More, the "developed" countries, but, in reality, the whole world. So it is worth reflecting a little on some topics less taken into account by the media, the socialists, the commentators and even the experts: the issues and themes of mental health and emotions in the case of pandemics . Because every biological pandemic also involves an **"emotional pandemic"** and a **"social pandemic".**

But also, every pandemic involves an "emotional pandemic" , some emotional components, and some social components, a "social pandemic" . The health of citizens is jeopardized (if not, there is no epidemic). But the mental or emotional stability of both individuals and groups and collectives is also more or less endangered . In addition, some epidemics can produce serious social disturbances or social changes.

One of the notable differences between this pandemic of COVID-19 and other pandemic in history consists precisely in the weight that the psychological and social components are having and in the speed of their influence.

Apparently, and from what we know so far, the disease that gives rise to its name as a pandemic(coronavirus-2019 disease), is a relatively mild disease manifested by cough, fever, general malaise and respiratory difficulties , and that only if there are other previous or concurrent pathologies can it be serious.

However, perhaps as never before in history, its worldwide psychological and social repercussions seem greater (or, at least, better known) than ever.

We come neurologically prepared for emotional communication : our brains and our psychology work by facilitating that massive transmission. And the existence of computerized social networks, the web, has only multiplied exponentially those emotional communication capacities of the species.

That is why the coronavirus crisis, apart from having made us aware of the reality of China as the first world power, forces us to rethink the planet and humanity as global , as a unitary whole.

Many thinkers these days have reflected on this seeming paradox: less biological danger but greater social danger, even with the danger of a widespread economic recession.

Let's imagine that the epidemic was spreading and that Europeans and North Americans wanted to flee it, taking advantage of COVID-19's apparent vulnerability to heat, trying to enter southern countries. What if they then denied us entry, as we have been doing with them for decades? What if they put walls, concertinas, police, armies, shells, gunshots, concentration camps ...? What would become of us and our possessions, weapons, wealth, consumer goods, relationships, memories, history ...? With the aggravating factor, above all, that, to a large extent, they are fleeing a social pandemic, not precisely a biological one, but directly caused by our "developed" countries: the weapons with which they kill and kill themselves, the weapons from which they flee , are made in our countries and contribute to our "well-being".

But there is another difference between this pandemic and other previous epidemics: that we can approach it with a different emotional and psychosocial perspective. In effect, what contributes the most to the severity of this epidemic, what turns it into a social crisis, is the emotional repercussion of it and how that emotional repercussion has invaded even those incorporeal but dominant entities that are "the markets" (after all, organizations and human beings dedicated to finance and related speculation).

And when it comes to emotions, today, as in previous epidemics, we tend to focus on fear, truly one of the species' basic, genetically pre-programmed human emotions. But today we know a little more about that subject, both from psychological and anthropological advances and from neuroscientific discoveries.

"Fear is a weapon of mass destruction"

Today we know, for example, that there are at least six other different emotional systems of fear , and that in all situations of catastrophe, stress or mourning they all start. Let's take the corona virus for an instance

Fear . We have been able to observe the implementation of fear and sometimes panic.

But also from anger (from some politicians to others, from some citizens to politicians or health workers, and from some citizens to others, as can be seen in computerized social networks).

Solidarity . We have been able to see outstanding flashes of the emotional system of solidarity, care and attachment (expansion of solidarity, attention to solidarity, dedication of health care professionals and other public workers ...).

Sadness. Possibly, we will see more and more sadness (for what we lose, for our previous mistakes, for the "feet of mud" and the extreme vulnerability of our world).

Wish . We will also be able to see (and enjoy) the delights of desire (after all, after each catastrophe or not very deadly social trap, nine months later there have been more births).

Inquiry. Every day we see in action the emotional system of inquiry, the interest in knowledge (in scientific research, in the desire to know about the disease, the epidemic and the world in which it developed, what China is really like, how is the world around us ...).

Joy. We have even seen the emotional system of joy and play develop (humor regarding our situation, use of humor to expand solidarity as in numerous videos and web communications, possibilities for other forms of play and joy).

All those massive emotional spreads are happening, and more than in other epidemics. Furthermore, we have more means, both conceptual and communication, to take this fact into account. Therefore it is not useful to use stigmatizing terms such as "mass hysteria" and "social psychosis".

We have to approach them as "massive emotional diffusions" (DEM), what we have called and studied as DEM, a subject in which precisely in Mediterranean countries we have a certain experience and renovating contributions from phenomena of this type experienced in many cities.

Using this other perspective can mean the possibility of preserving and developing mental health even in a crisis situation , such as the one we are undoubtedly experiencing.

For example, we must consider that the phrase "letting oneself be carried away by emotions" on a social level is not scientifically applicable in these cases , repeating over and over that the population "is letting themselves be carried away by emotions": it will be by emotions "Dissociative" (fear, anger) instead of the binding.

Or not even that: the real problem is getting carried away by the manipulation of emotions . In reality, we all let ourselves be carried away by emotions and more on a social level.

Emotions are our first way of knowing and reacting in the world and, therefore, we must use them in the mental health care of populations.

Let's see some consequences. Communications, knowledge, data are not enough to guide the social response to the pandemic . Cognitions are not enough. It is not enough to attack and criticize the "emotionality" (of others). This would be a first consequence.

And the people stayed at home": the viral poem about the pandemic

We must complement the use of cognitions, information, knowledge and data, with the use of binding, solidarity emotions such as: attachment-care (the basis of solidarity), interest, desire, sadness for the previous mistakes, joy and humor ...

Perhaps that is more difficult than disseminating data and knowledge alone, but it is also more realistic, more effective, and more based on current scientific perspectives . This is well known, in a negative sense, by the usual manipulators of public opinion and advertising in the media.

Linking in solidarity is: caring for caregivers, highlighting and cultivating solidarity, caring for the elderly and the vulnerable ...

Bonding in that regard, and not just out of fear. It is a good time to get closer to films (such as Humana), Games, Books And Audiovisuals That Stimulate Solidarity.

10 Keys To Overcome The Emotional pandemic.

What can we do in times of emotional turbulence? A lot of solidarity, caring and caring for ourselves, not getting used to the emotional distance ... And taking advantage to learn from all the lessons that this crisis brought us.

Luckily, positive and binding emotions are just as contagious as fear, we review everything that each and everyone can do to overcome these times of emotional turbulence.

1. **Stimulate Solidarity And Responsibility, As A Group, And Avoid Isolating Yourself Personally**

It is a good time to reflect on how important it is to be part of a group , a social network, a family or other identities. As soon as the crisis is over, or even earlier, reflect on how to improve those linkages.

2. **Bet On The Protection Offered By Health And Production, Distribution And Exchange Services That Are Social**

Work on its development and regulation. For example, teleworking will now develop more and more, which can mean greater autonomy of management and thought.

3. **Take Care Of Our Caregivers: Do Not Make Non-Urgent Or Unnecessary Consultations**

Consulting again and again or at the slightest discomfort or symptom on health phones and / or health services hinders its function. There are public and easily accessible lists of the fundamental symptoms of pandemic, both on the computerized network, in newspapers and in health centers. Read them and learn them. And if you have questions, look among your family and friends who can help you (by phone or remotely). Remember that we have a European and national treasure: efficient public health that must be cared for.

4. **Grooming And Dressing Each Day, Not Giving Up On Those Aspects**

Make a daily and weekly schedule and stick to it. Include moments of communication with the family through computerized social networks. You can watch films and videos of laughter (and other types), share board games, sports, outdoor activities and nature - if the situation allows. At least every two hours, do physical exercises according to a program, there are many on the Internet.

5. Take Advantage To Lower The Pace Of Life And Consumption

It is a good time to remember that a third of some children in some part of the world are poorly fed, 13% go hungry, there are thousands of people sleeping on the streets, there are hundreds of thousands of people with housing difficulties and serious relational disturbances in the home, Millions of people with a precarious job ... How important are social services in a state of solidarity ! Collaborate in reflecting on the topic. How can I help keep them running?

Often, we delegate too many things to school, tutors and centers for extracurricular activities, sports, games and summer, teachers ... What we are missing! You can take advantage of it to see how to "build the world in a better way".

7. Let Yourself Be Carried Away By The Interest Of Solidarity Knowledge And Inquiry

It is a good time to rethink the world and move towards radical environmentalism and humanism. . Also, to rethink everyday consumerism and see how to have "more time with children" and more time for other activities and solidarity, recreational and joyful perspectives.

8. The Evaluation Of Formal And Daily Democracy

It is the fundamental contribution of Europe to the world: at the service of the majority and with respect and cultivation of critical minorities and differences . The combination of democracy and solidarity states, at the service of those most in need, is another characteristic European contribution. Our way out of the crisis must be based on these premises.

In a short brief, let's quickly move into Psychoneuroimmunology and it's Interrelation between the nervous, endocrine and immune systems.

Disease is often the result of the interaction of multiple factors, an interaction that takes place mainly through the nervous, endocrine and immune systems. This chapter addresses so-called psychoneuroimmunology, as a branch of science that studies the complex interrelationships between the central nervous system and the immune system.

Since time immemorial, the association between situations of physical and psychological stress with the genesis of diseases, especially infections, has been observed. Not in vain already in 400 BC Hippocrates made the tandem "Healthy mind in healthy body" popular.

During the last decades, a great deal of information has been accumulating that supports the hypothesis that the nervous and endocrine systems play an important role in the pathophysiology of diseases that affect the immune system, including infectious processes, cancer and autoimmune diseases. Initially, factors related to the nervous system (including psychosocial factors) were thought to play a prominent role in the etiology of autoimmune processes, however, more recent studies indicate that these factors interact with other clinically important determinants, among which are They include genetic factors and exposure to pathogens, which determine the course and prognosis of the disease.

Currently, it is admitted that the interaction between the central nervous system and the organism is much more dynamic than initially believed, since there are a series of substances that, starting from the immune system, are capable of altering psychological and neurological functions. , acting both centrally and peripherally, which suggests that communication between the two systems is bi-directional.

"Every living being experiences and requires stress, as it allows it to

adapt to new conditions, on occurring occasions".

Finally, the aforementioned interaction between the immune system and the nervous system cannot be ignored, since the cells of the former are influenced by the central and peripheral nervous system, giving rise to the production by the immune system of the so-called cytokines, which have the capacity to alter neuronal activity, influencing the different bio-psychological processes. Thus the exciting field of psychoneuroimmunology arises, although it would be more appropriate to speak of psychoneuroendocrinoimmunology, as will be seen below.

<u>Integrating Discipline</u>

Psychoneuroimmunology is a discipline that brings together researchers from numerous medical specialties, such as neuroscience, immunology, physiology, pharmacology, psychiatry, psychology, behavioral sciences, rheumatology, and infectious diseases. It is responsible for studying the interactions between the immune system, behavior, the central nervous system and the endocrine system.

As a parcel of knowledge it presents a fairly recent development, since for a long time it was believed that the immune system was an exclusively self-regulating system.

The different research works carried out in the field of psychoneuroimmunology allow the following conclusions to be drawn:

The cells of the immune system express receptors for numerous molecules regulated mainly by the central nervous system: adrenergic receptors (a and b), dopaminergic receptors, serotonergic receptors, and histaminergic receptors, among others.

The identification of fibers of the central nervous system in the lymphatic tissues shows the existence of a direct communication between the central nervous system and the immune system.

Studies in experimental animals have shown through lesions in regions of the central nervous system that the regulation of the immune system corresponds to the brain.

The interconnection between the immune system and the central nervous system is also evident in the fact that learning processes influence the immune system, conditioning it, either enhancing or reducing it.

The conclusions just presented support the existence of complex mechanisms of interaction and communication between the nervous, endocrine and immune systems. This communication uses a biochemical language in which substances produced by the systems themselves intervene: neurotransmitters, hormones and cytokines, respectively.

Psychoneuro Immunology And Disease

The beliefs and value system of each individual allow them to process stress-generating situations, which depending on those beliefs and those values can be translated into diverse feelings (fear, anger, depression, helplessness, hopelessness), inputs Negatives that act biochemically, activating various mechanisms, including the axis formed by the hypothalamus, the pituitary, and the adrenal glands. Activation of the aforementioned mechanisms can suppress or reduce the response of the immune system, which in turn allows pathological conditions of diverse nature to develop, one of which is cancer.

The results from experimental studies and clinical observations allow us to conclude that diseases are the result of the interaction between multiple factors, which depend both on the offending agent (bacteria, viruses, carcinogens), and on the attacked organism (genetic, nervous characteristics, endocrine, emotional, immunological, cognitive and behavioral, age, gender, life experiences and psychosocial factors). All these data offer great possibilities from the clinical perspective, since they offer the possibility of considering psychological treatment as support for pharmacological treatment, or even as preventive treatment of the disease.

<u>Stress</u>

Stress can be defined as any stimulus that is perceived as a threat to the homeostasis and security of the individual. When the stimulus persists, tolerance develops, while if it is very intense, it decomposes the subject (it may even cause death).

Since it constitutes a mechanism of psychological and organic adaptation to changes in the internal and external environment, stress is universal and inherent in living beings. There are different types of stress:

- Physical (trauma, surgery, burns, infection).
- Psychological (interpersonal problems, upsets, exams).
- Metabolic (hemorrhages, dehydration, hypoglycemia, ketoacidosis).
- Pharmacological (amphetamines, cocaine).

Every living being experiences and requires stress, since it allows them to adapt to new conditions, sometimes injurious. Stress also affects viruses and bacteria.

In the stress response three phases are distinguished: alarm or reaction, adaptation and de-compensation. The first two phases are part of the everyday and beneficial for life, producing a slight increase in stress hormones, at the same time that organic functions improve in order to adapt or triumph over stressful challenges. The de-compensation phase is characterized by its negativity, favoring the development of acute, chronic and fatal pathologies. Factors such as genetics and previous traumatic experiences of the individual influence tolerance and adaptation to stress.

Immune Response

Innate or nonspecific immunity and specific or acquired immunity are the two components that, properly communicated, constitute the immune system. In turn, specific immunity includes two subtypes: humoral immunity, represented by antibodies produced by B lymphocytes, and cellular immunity, mediated by T lymphocytes .

Specific immunity.

The immune response is initiated by cells of the nonspecific system (neutrophils, macrophages, and dendritic cells), which phagocytize the germs and then present antigens to helper T lymphocytes (T CD4). These lymphocytes decide whether specific humoral immunity or cellular specific immunity will act.

Intercellular contact and so-called cytokines allow communication between the different components of the immune system, as well as modulation of their response.

Cytokines are low molecular weight glycoproteins, generated by activation of the immune system, capable of binding to specific receptors present on the cell surface, in order to modify the gene expression pattern of target cells. Currently almost 200 cytokines are known whose biological actions and origins are very varied. In general, cytokines act in cascade, regulating processes such as hematopoiesis, proliferation, cell differentiation, and apoptosis.

Stress And Immunity

Studies on the effects of stress suggest that stress can alter the immune system, leading to the appearance of infectious, oncological or autoimmune processes, processes that are due to an inhibition of the immune response. The ability of the body to adapt to the stimulus affects the immune response, thus conditioning the individual response to infection, cancer, etc. It should be remembered that at certain stages of life (fetal, perinatal and senescence), the stress-immunity interaction becomes more important.

On the other hand, during stress neurotransmitters and hormones are released, most of which have receptors and activity on immune cells. Thus, for example, corticosteroids inhibit a large number of pro inflammatory cytokines.

In general, it can be said that a stressful event affects the immune system in two ways:

- Causing changes in the distribution of cells in the body, which influences the local response to a pathogen.
- Altering the cellular response itself.

Clinical Impact Of Immune Alterations Generated By Stress

Severe stress, both acute and chronic, profoundly influences susceptibility and the evolution of acute and chronic pathologies, since it induces disorders in immunoregulation, and specifically, in immunoregulatory cytokine chains.

The clinical pictures that are associated with stress include infections, trauma, cancer, allergy, autoimmunity and psychiatric diseases.

As already mentioned, the communication between the immune system and the central nervous system is bidirectional and begins already in the embryo itself, where a large number of immunoregulatory molecules appear, such as tumor necrosis factor a. This communication is maintained throughout life, demonstrating the neuropsychological effects of cytokines, immune activation, and the immunomodulatory effects of the neuroendocrine system. This is the reason why there are currently numerous investigations in progress on the effects exerted by cytokines in inflammatory, neuropsychological and degenerative diseases, so that the study of the effect of stress in pathologies such as depression, schizophrenia,

Trauma

Critically ill polytraumatized patients have been shown to usually present anergic symptoms (characterized by sudden fatigue or fatigue, often related to a drop in defenses), and are even more susceptible to bacterial and infectious processes. opportunistic fungal, which is due to defects in innate, cellular and humoral immunity.

In relation to the skin and mucosa, especially with regard to the gastrointestinal mucosa, immunity is affected by the reduction in the number of B lymphocytes and in the production of immunoglobulin A (IgA), which results in delayed healing of surgical and traumatic wounds.

It is currently known that in polytraumatized and critically ill patients, the secretion of cytokines fluctuates enormously, going from a state with a predominantly proinflammatory state in which the production of interleukin 1, tumor necrosis factor a, interleukin 2 and interferon g, stands out to another of character anti-inflammatory with a predominance of interleukins 4 and 10. It is recognized that the interaction between pro-inflammatory cytokines and anti-inflammatory cytokines conditions immune dysfunctions, as well as the prognosis of the patient.

Excess proinflammatory cytokines cause the most frequent and lethal complications in critically injured and critically ill patients: acute respiratory failure and organic multisystem failure. On the contrary, the deficiencies of the mentioned cytokines, together with an excess of the anti-inflammatory cytokines, is associated with a state of anergy to cutaneous antigens, which leads to a situation of severe cellular immunodeficiency.

The results of some experimental studies indicate that interferon g and adrenergic agonists b impair the formation of interleukin 10, which translates into an increase in cellular immunity, thus improving the prognosis of critically ill humans and animals.

The immune system is currently believed to be a sensory organ that scans the internal environment to discover infection and trauma and inform the central nervous system. It is then when the latter elaborates endocrine and neurotransmitter messages that regulate the immune response, thus avoiding inflammatory immune hyperactivity that can harm the host. Thus, intense stress, both physical and psychological, alters the immune system in several ways:

Favoring the development of opportunistic infections due to quantitative and functional or qualitative cellular immunodeficiency.

Participating in or promoting the development of symptoms of acute inflammatory origin, due to alteration of cytokine chains.

Favoring the development of diseases as diverse as Alzheimer's and autoimmune pathologies, the etiology of which is believed to be influenced by stress-induced cytokine disorders.

Producing viral reactivation, which could be the consequence of intense chronic and acute stress.

Infectious Processes

Stress induces an immunodeviation of cytokines, a process that seems to influence powerfully the evolution of infectious diseases, especially those produced by intracellular germs combated by Th1 cellular immunity, natural killer cytotoxic cells, CD4 and CD8. Viral processes, tuberculosis, leprosy, syphilis, fungal infections, parasitic diseases and tumors, especially those associated with infections, are included here. Viral infections, and especially those of persistent viruses such as those in the herpes group, are known to show reactivation during stress, together with or simultaneously with functional and quantitative immune disorders. An inefficient immune response to viral vaccines administered to people in stress has also been demonstrated.

HIV infection deserves special mention, in which cytokines have been shown to be involved, for example, in the progression of infection from the asymptomatic state to acquired immunodeficiency syndrome (AIDS), cachexia, metabolic wasting syndrome, and genesis of tumors. The few patients who experience spontaneous improvement in HIV infection owe it to various factors that promote the development of specific anti-HIV immunity with CD8 cells.

Currently, there is evidence, both biological and clinical, that corroborates the existing suspicions about the importance of stressors of the psychosocial, emotional and traumatic type, in the acceleration of the progression towards AIDS.

Autoimmune Diseases And Allergy

The effect of stress on autoimmune processes is extremely complex. It can exacerbate in some cases and improve in others the symptoms of the various autoimmune disorders.

On the other hand, the hypo and hyperactive states of the stress axis (hypothalamic / pituitary / adrenal axis), which are abundant in the human clinic, must be taken into account. Suppression of corticosteroid therapy, immediate postpartum, chronic fatigue syndrome, Addison's disease and premenstrual tension, among others, are considered hypoactive states. Hyperactive stress systems are seen in chronic stress, alcoholism and withdrawal syndrome, depression, malnutrition, exaggerated exercise and the first trimester of pregnancy, among others.

Cancer

Certain mood states such as depression have been associated with the genesis and evolution of malignant processes. The immune response has been shown to be correlated with cancer survival.

It is known that stress favors the development of neoplasms, mainly due to alterations in immunoregulation and DNA that affect its repair mechanisms. There is evidence showing that stressed subjects are more vulnerable to environmental toxins, both immune and genetic.

Psychiatric Diseases

In relation to psychiatric disorders, cytokines seem to play an important role in pathologies such as schizophrenia and Alzheimer's disease. Regarding the latter, an increase in interleukins 1 and 6 has been observed, which in turn have been correlated with increases in the synthesis of amyloid proteins, which is why they can be considered one of the determining factors of this disease.

When addressing the relationship between psychiatric disorders and the immune system, it is observed that depression has been the most studied disease in this area, with a decrease in the activity of natural killer cells and in the response to mitogens being observed in its development . On the other hand, the severity of the depression, the age and the sex of the affected person also influence the functioning of the immune system. The alterations found in depressed patients could be explained by the alteration in the secretion of cortisol, a substance that plays an important role in the functioning of the immune system.

In another order of things, it is widely accepted that the most consistent biological marker in depression is sleep disturbance, and especially early awakening. In addition, sleep-related problems are very present in the symptoms of diseases such as fibromyalgia and chronic fatigue, to which must be added the current rhythm of life, which substantially modifies the quality and total quantity of sleep. Precisely another factor that also affects immune function is the wake / sleep rhythm.

Psychological Effect On Mental Health

Let's take for instance a situation like the COVID-19 pandemic causes anxiety and fear, which affects our mental health. Some recommendations that the WHO has made to minimize this effect. In this sense, we can reduce the time spent watching, reading or listening to news that causes anxiety or distress, we can set specific times to report, for example, twice a day. It is important to seek information from reliable sources, mainly measures that help protect against the virus; Ignoring rumors or misinformation, and only following reliable information helps lessen fear. You have to protect yourself and provide support to others, "working together as a single community can help create solidarity by tackling COVID-19 together," says WHO. Maintaining optimism can be helped by giving visibility to positive and encouraging stories and images of people who have recovered or cared for a loved one. Let us recognize the importance of people who care for others and of health workers who are dealing with the pandemic.

What factors can affect my mental health?

The mental health is an integral part of health and wellness. This means that, as a society, we must have strategies for the prevention, treatment and recovery of pandemic diseases that affect our mental health.

"Health is a state of physical, mental and social well-being, it is not only the absence of disease or illness": WHO

The range of mental disorders that exist is very wide, however the most common are:

- Organic mental disorders (Alzheimer, vascular dementia, senile dementia, etc.).
- Mental disorders due to substance use (alcohol or drugs).
- Psychotic disorders (Schizophrenia, schizotypal disorder, etc).
- Affective disorders (bipolar disorder, depressive disorder, mania, etc).
- Anxiety disorders (phobias, obsessive-compulsive disorder, post-traumatic stress,
- dissociative disorders, etc.).
- Behavioral disorders (eating disorders, sleep disorders, etc.).
- Personality disorders (histrionics, narcissism, etc.).

Depression in a disease that affects the physical, emotional, intellectual, spiritual and social spheres of those who suffer from it. It is a health problem, not a problem of will.

The origin of a depressive state is multifactorial, but there are certain predisposing factors for it to occur. These factors are biological, psychological, and social.

The physical causes have to do with genetic inheritance, hormonal alterations or brain chemistry. Psychological factors have to do with personality traits, losses, mourning processes and circumstantial or developmental crises, for example adolescence, the "arrival of the forties", menopause or the stage of retirement. Social causes are closely linked to psychological causes and are frequently related to dysfunctional family dynamics, having been the victim of some type of sexual, physical or psychological abuse, having experienced traumatic events, the constant experience of some type of uncertainty, for example economic or security (violent cities or high crime rates), a complex for a physical disability or living in a hostile environment with constant aggression.

All of the above is basically manifested in a condition that causes alterations in brain biochemistry and in the processes of regulation in mood. Thus, depression is defined as a mood disorder characterized by feelings of despondency, unhappiness, low self-esteem, loss of interest and the ability to enjoy daily activities. Depression significantly affects our well-being and our relationship with the environment.

Depression is not a temporary state of mind, its symptoms settle for a period longer than six weeks and therefore affect the quality of life of those who suffer from it.

When we are depressed nothing looks good, it doesn't sound the same, it doesn't feel nice, or it looks fun. Depression is a tyrant, a little monster that takes over our lives and forces us to dig an increasingly dark and black hole within our existence. But depression is hell that doesn't last forever. Everything ends up happening. The good thing about the bad is that it ends ... Depression is curable.

And what has to be done when the disease has been identified?

It is necessary to go immediately to a specialist, because it has been observed that depression rarely remits on its own. This means that it is a disease that requires constant and committed professional treatment, because the symptoms are always on the increase, and rarely decrease on their own.

A depressive state, although it is a disease, does not have to be permanent. It is controllable, and when the symptoms recede, the vision clears and everything begins to be seen with more serenity and more light.

Depression can be treated with psychotherapy, medical treatment, and joint treatment. Only a specialist doctor, clinical psychologist or psychiatrist will be able to decide which is the best treatment.

In the case of post-traumatic stress disorder, according to WHO studies, 3.6% of the world population suffered it last year. The study points out that, of the respondents, 21% witnessed acts of violence, 18.8% suffered interpersonal violence, 17.7% were involved in accidents, 16.2 were exposed to warfare and 12.5% suffered traumatic events related to beloved.

Conclusion

Every pandemic involves changes and dangers at the biological, psychological and social levels . Now we realize more clearly than ever. Until now, almost thirty centuries after the birth of scientific medicine, we thought, and with reason, that the dangers were primarily biological. And it is like this: the term pandemic must be circumscribed to its biological realities, that is, to the danger that it represents for the life and health of citizens, and the world at large.

CHAPTER THREE:

MENTAL HEALTH PROTECTION IN PANDEMIC SITUATIONS

Let's take for instance in the circumstances of the coronavirus pandemic, adaptive and non-adaptive psychological reactions inevitably arise. The aim of this Health Charter is to show the psychological aspects that arise due to the events related to the pandemic and to give recommendations to face them.

In the initial part, the document is presented in two columns, the first is a story that aims to exemplify behaviors, emotions and sensations with which a person can be identified, and the second shows the explanation of the psychological phenomena that are intuited in each story paragraph; psychological phenomena that must be learned to identify and manage, to avoid them becoming non-adaptive, dysfunctional or pathological reactions.

A story...

At the end of December last year, Silvia was preparing to celebrate the new year, for which she bought salad, cake and soda at the supermarket. She was very happy that she would reunited with her parents, uncles, cousins and grandmother. On her way home, she turned on the radio in her car and heard the following news: "Doctor Li Wenliang from Wuhan China suggests that you be careful of a contagious disease that starts like a flu and ends in pneumonia." At that moment, Silvia thought, "Wuhan? China? It is very far!... Furthermore, Science has progressed a lot and soon they will find a treatment. She changed stations and played music.

In mid-January Silvia remembered the news heard in December, she had almost forgotten it. A friend told him that the doctor Li Wenliang, who first diagnosed the presence of the infection in Wuhan, had died of pneumonia caused by the coronavirus, the disease discovered by him.

Alarm increased when she began to see on the news the progress of the epidemic and the deaths caused. First in China, then in Italy, later in Spain, also in Switzerland and Germany. Silvia was scared to think that the pandemic would come to Colombia and the risk that it meant for her father, her uncles, her grandmother or the doctors, who remain most of the time in hospitals.

Progressively the word coronavirus became everyday, someone always had something to say, a comment, sometimes wrapped in humor.

When the first case was reported in Colombia, Silvia began to feel anxiety; her heart began to race, she felt discomfort in her chest, physical exhaustion and upset stomach. She could not concentrate on her activities, her world was saturated with information about COVID-19, in a sieve of despair and fear. Her gastrointestinal symptoms increased, she lost her appetite, she became certain that something serious was happening in the world, in her country, in her neighborhood, that it could happen at home and to herself. She began to feel the foreign and strange world; she had episodes of crying, sometimes irritability and short temper combined with anxiety and sadness.

Declared quarantine and the government's order to stay home, Silvia understood that the pandemic was definitely a reality in her country. She tried to organize her time and adjust to the situation of being at home continuously with her parents. Now she feels moments of anxiety and sadness, sometimes she becomes irritable, but she has discovered that she must be patient and that it is best to follow the instructions of the scientists and the authorities. Silvia presents a lot of uncertainty (not being able to predict what will happen); There is nothing clear in front of the panorama and she asks herself: when will I be able to leave my house without feeling insecure and in danger? Will what happened in Italy happen here? Will I get sick? Will I die? will any of my relatives die?

An explanation...

Human beings have personal resources to protect themselves from adversity and, as an adaptation strategy, they involve thoughts, emotions and actions to adapt to new situations (pleasant, threatening, unforeseen, etc.). The mind devises amazing ways to explain and evaluate situations.

In general, what is interpreted as dangerous to life or psychological stability is perceived as "a threatening event", in response to which a feeling of absence of internal resources to successfully deal with it may be experienced.

A piece of news that apparently is not important acquires another relevance when it is commented again and expanded; If it is something that does not affect the integrity of the human being or some other aspect of life, it tends not to be important. But if the information continues to be presented, it is permanently established in people's knowledge, accentuated by involving situations of suffering or adversity.

The context of this epidemic, which evolved into a pandemic, generates fears that determine certain behaviors of control, protection or evasion when the probability of affecting one's life and that of those close to it is perceived. Here, experiences appear between the consideration of danger and the perception of unreality (as a mental control or protection strategy).

The need for adaptation leads to trying to normalize, minimize or maximize the information received, in order to have time to assimilate what is happening. This is why jokes and memes are used with the aim of appeasing the imminent perception of danger. People laugh at the tragedy as a way to tolerate a dramatic reality. But the situation in the world every time

it becomes more threatening, therefore feelings of vulnerability and persecution of an invisible enemy arise. In these threatening situations for physical or psychological integrity, neurobiological systems equivalent to fear and anxiety are activated in the body, producing a hyper-alert state that can manifest physiologically with acceleration of the heart, restlessness, increased breathing, sleep disturbance, of appetite, among others.

It is normal to feel fear and anxiety about the current contingency, which can be increased by uncertainty, but strategies must be generated to control these feelings. If these strategies are not created, mental health can be threatened. If the invasion of fear is allowed, the measures taken are not fully accepted, we continuously regret the things that were wanted to be done and could not be done, if it is not possible to take active control of this new reality, there will be no rest, nor tranquility. The body will continually release adrenaline and cortisol, which while helping at adaptation, can cause, over the weeks, abnormal depression or anxiety.

In a pandemic situation like the current one, three components that generate anxiety come together: the threat to life, the change of daily routines and uncertainty. It is not possible to live a pandemic without fear; Mental health professionals, in this situation, have also felt fear, going through moments of unease, frustration, uncertainty and hopelessness.

At other times, feelings of hope, acceptance and compensation arise, thinking, for example, that this is a lesson for humanity and, after the crisis is over, the appreciation that one will have of life, fellow human beings and planet, it will be different. Some of the strategies that can be put in place to cope with these times of pandemic are briefly described below :

Talk about the topic: it is common to feel the need to comment on what is thought or what is felt as a result of the pandemic, the economic crisis and the social repercussions. Concerns are exposed, positive and negative things are discussed. Talking produces a psychological effect called catharsis, which consists of the elaboration of emotional tensions through the verbalization of tragic situations.

Think about what you are thinking about: all people have the ability to think about what they are thinking and thus can control mental processes. This is an innate ability of human beings and is called metacognition. If the person thinks that their grandmother is going to die in the pandemic, this is a catastrophic, non-adaptive and stress-generating thought, especially if all the recommended measures are being taken so that she does not become infected. This person has the ability to analyze her thinking and choose to relate to it but in a different way, opting for alternatives that involve less anxiety and lead to more effective behaviors. You should constantly review what you think, measure its magnitude and give reason; in this way, it avoids distressingly overvaluing adversity and can be evaluated in its concrete and just measure.

Identify and accept what you are feeling: although distressing emotions arise spontaneously in threatening situations, such as those that can be experienced in this pandemic, recognizing them allows them to be regulated. In addition to being able to breathe consciously (pay attention and describe the breath), use meditation techniques, listen to soothing music, talk to friends and family, it is important to try to verify the facts (describe them without the presence of value judgments) to define whether the Emotion experienced adjusts to the situation or not. The more the facts can be objectively described, the less emotional overflow will be experienced.

Use your time appropriately: apply the rule of eight: 8 hours of sleep

Sleep can be disturbed in a pandemic situation, which is why it is important to strictly follow Sleep Hygiene standards:

- Establish a defined time to go to sleep and get up.
- Take a maximum 45 minute nap.
- Avoid heavy food four hours before sleeping.
- Avoid coffee, chocolate or dark drinks in the afternoon or evening.
- Avoid liquor, don't smoke.

- Exercise, hopefully in the morning, never before bed.
- Wear comfortable and soft clothing.
- Have the room at a suitable temperature and also ventilated.
- Turn off the TV and all sources of noise before falling asleep.
- Use the bed to sleep, avoid working on it.

Last recommendation: when you want to fall asleep, avoid thinking that you have to sleep, sleep is an automatic phenomenon. Many people do not fall asleep because they think they have to sleep, this causes them anguish. Wanting to fall asleep, you can follow the sequence of a nice story or movie, pray, count sheep, etc.

8 hours of work and development of other compulsory activities

- Avoid staying in pajamas all day, shortly after getting up, it is important to try to bathe and dress even if you do not leave your home.
- Build a schedule of mandatory activities, telecommuting or online work and stick to it. Include domestic activities in this period.
- Use the cell phone in a regulated way; save or silence it during periods of work and compulsory activities.
- Stay informed through trusted and recognized sources. Do not obsess over information, watch the news or get information once or twice a day, for periods no longer than half an hour.
- Strictly comply with the recommendations of the health authorities; if you exhaustively comply with the recommendations, the possibility of contagion, for you or your family, approaches zero.

8 hours of pleasant and playful activities

- Make feeding periods a pleasant opportunity to share and try new recipes.
- Listen to music, sing, and do karaoke.

- Use social networks and calls as a strategy to share with your family and friends. Go back to relationships you had neglected. Discard contacts that send alarming or intimidating information.
- Exercise 3 or 4 times a week; online you will find tutorials to do routines at home.
- Watching movies or series with your family, playing cards, parquet flooring, dominoes. Online they offer thousands of individual or family entertainment activities.
- Read books and discuss them with those close to you.
- Make a seedbed and a home garden, this will give you a lot of satisfaction and the seeds come spontaneously to the kitchen. Sow vegetables and legumes. It is not necessary to have a patio, it can be done in flowerpots in a bright place in the house or apartment.
- Organizing, painting or fixing the house is an opportunity that gives confinement.

Important

If you have a history of a disorder that has required psychiatric care, it is important to be alert. It is necessary to differentiate very well between the normal adaptive reaction and the symptomatic relapse.

CHAPTER FOUR:

CONTEMPORARY METHODS FOR MAINTAINING PANDEMICS

Since the origin of their own existence, human beings have been exposed to various risks, associated with natural catastrophes, accidents, as well as diseases and health pandemic; However, from the 60s to the 20th century, with the emergence of nuclear energy and, consequently, the risks that the use of this type of energy implies in terms of safety, society was exposed to new risks associated with the scientific-technological development achieved.

METHOD 1: RISK COMMUNICATON

These new risks transgress territorial, ethnic and membership limits to social groups, and all societies are equally endangered, regardless of their ideology and levels of economic development, even though both factors affect the ways of dealing with such risks.

In these situations, communication began to give them different treatment as part of risk management, hence the present work is focused on risk communication for the control of public health emergencies, with emphasis on the preventive or pre-stage -crisis of the emergency; feature that differs from crisis communication, which is aimed at safeguarding the image of the organization before its public if it is going through a crisis.

This chapter supports the need for health risk communication as a permanent practice of the health system to face public emergency situations, where the role of risk communication strategies is highlighted, which from their effective implementation will contribute to elevate the perception of risk in the target audiences and, consequently, to minimize the negative effects of health emergencies in material and human life terms.

The predominant theoretical approaches in relation to risk communication in the health context were taken as a starting point, its development from health emergency experiences led by the World Health Organization (WHO), where the risk communication strategy is highlighted as a key tool to mitigate the effects of public health emergencies.

Risk communication in its theoretical-practical evolution has been influenced by different theories, models and approaches from Sociology, Psychology, Economics, and Social Education, just to mention the most referenced in the scientific literature and with the greatest impact in health practices aimed at the prevention of health risks.

The following were identified as fundamental analytical perspectives: the psychological perspective, the scientific-economic perspective, the sociological perspective or sociocultural paradigm and the Peter Sandman model. In these the relationship between communication and risk is analyzed from the objective and / or subjective nature established between the two.

From a psychological perspective, communication management focuses on risk perception and the factors that influence the intensity of perceived risk or not, in relation to real risk. Among the most studied factors, there are catastrophic potential, familiarity, understanding, scientific uncertainty, perception of control, voluntary exposure and impact on children, and that other factors, such as terror, institutional trust, accident history, risk benefits, reversibility and personal interests, among others. This perspective weighs subjective risk and finds its counterpart in the scientific-economic approach.

In this regard, the scientific-economic perspective starts from the need to socialize scientific and technological advances to all of society, by the academic community. Initially, this need was related to the use of nuclear energy, and approaches that started from considering a risk-benefit ratio of a quantifiable nature in economic terms and that consequently imply the acceptance of risks in exchange for significant economic benefits prevailed.

This approach tilts the balance towards objective risk, but "... what individuals or societies perceive as risk, and decide to assume it that way, cannot be reduced to objective criteria ...". For this reason, sometimes the balance also shifts by weighing subjective risk when these issues are submitted to citizen approval as part of the public agenda of governments.

Public perception can be differentiated from scientific perception of risk, because it is not based only on objective data; Rather, the frameworks for public perception of risk are often based on subjective criteria or unscientific sources, and are not always as reliable, such as political decisions, dominant beliefs, and the information provided by the media, which to a large extent Significant factors condition the real perception of risk, even more than the scientific evaluation .

In the sociological perspective or sociocultural paradigm, risk is conceived from "social constructions that depend on sociocultural factors linked to given social structures". In this sense, risk only exists as representation; and some scholars take it for granted that "the perception and acceptance of risks have their roots in social and cultural factors".

With this perspective, sociocultural factors are highlighted as determining the way in which a risk is perceived by the different social groups and their role in the changes in its perception and in the ability to respond to hazards. Therefore, it is considered that the response to the same risk may vary in different cultural contexts.

In addition, supporting studies during emergency situations, in which the relationship between perceived risk and real risk play a determining role, as "the dangers that kill people and the risks that alarm them are different " and the criterion that" people respond only to the risks they perceive ".

The fundamental components are risk = danger + risk perception, and it is analyzed in four moments: low danger-high perception, high danger-low perception, high danger-high perception and moderate danger-moderate perception. In each one, the population's response to danger is analyzed and, correspondingly, it will be the treatment from risk communication.

The risks are made known to the population through scientific dissemination, from non-governmental organizations, from the public agendas of governments at their different levels, from the media and from social networks through authorized voices in the topic; These last two become key mediating supports in the crisis and post-crisis stages during the emergency.

Communication, undoubtedly, would have an essential function not only in the risk management stages, but also in the process of building the social representation of a certain risk and in fixing it in society, particularly for risk groups and vulnerable communities.

It should be noted, as a distinctive feature of risk communication, that it places emphasis on risk prevention because it will depend on how to face the crisis stage by the target public; unlike crisis communication, which acts to protect the image, operation and reputation of the organization vis-à-vis its audiences in the face of a certain internal crisis.

Health Risk Communication In Health Emergencies

Health emergency situations have been institutionally managed from communication, as an essential part of risk management, since the 1980s of the last century, where experiences in the control of these health events have allowed us to define and redefine nature of risk communication.

Initially, communication in emergency situations and pandemic outbreaks was defined as "an interactive process of exchange of information and opinion among people, groups and institutions; it usually includes multiple messages about the nature of the risk or expresses concerns, opinions or reactions about the messages about risk or legal and institutional arrangements for risk management. "

Already in the 21st century the experiences of international health emergencies allowed to redefine health risk communication "... as the decision-making process that takes into account political, social and economic factors, which analyzes risk as a potential danger in order formulating, studying and comparing control options with a view to selecting the best response for the safety of the population in the face of probable danger, attaches great importance to dialogue with affected populations and with the interested public, in order to provide them with the necessary information , that allows them to make the best possible decisions during an emergency or disaster with an impact on public health. "

This definition of the WHO, gathers the experiences of this organization before epidemic emergencies in the last decades, and has been appropriated by regional health entities such as the Pan American Health Organization, the International Red Cross, the Red Crescent, among others. At the same time, it is part of the foundations that govern the standards established by the International Health Regulations (IHR) for situations of public health emergencies, which are strictly complied with by the different states and governments that accept this.

Risk communication is recognized as the basic capacity No. 6 of the RSI, which includes the following activities:

- Identification of collaborators and allies.
- Formation of a team in charge of public communications with defined functions in the event of a public health event.
- Identification and training of spokespersons to respond quickly (be timely in communicating news and providing regular updates).
- Preparation of special communication plans for certain situations, which include public information and social mobilization.
- Ability to establish criteria to disclose information to the public in consultation with technical-scientific personnel and authorities, before disclosing the information.
- Validation of special plans.
- Planning and executing evaluations of the risk communication component after a public health event, which will include the evaluation of transparency, the relevance of the messages, the first announcement in the first 24 hours that follow the confirmation of the event.
- Planning to include the lessons learned in the operational plans after the evaluation of the events.
- Updating of information channels with the community and the media, such as websites, community meetings, radio broadcasts at national and local levels, among others.

The activities that risk communication develops within the framework of the IHR are necessary for the different phases of an emergency with an impact on public health; For which it is important to have authorities and professionals in charge, duly trained to make decisions, who will contribute to maintaining the confidence of the population in its management and in the recommendations to quickly control the episode.

A key experience for the development of risk communication in the health field was in 2004 the epidemic of severe acute respiratory syndrome, which together with the increase in outbreaks of emerging diseases, in addition to experiences in disaster emergencies, led to that the WHO develop, in consultation with experts, the 5 communication norms or essential practices to face epidemic outbreaks and health emergencies, which are presented below:

1. Trust

It constitutes the essential principle of communication in situations of pandemic outbreak. Communication must generate, maintain or regain confidence in the event of a crisis between citizens and managers throughout the health emergency. Trust will guarantee credibility in messages issued by national authorities.

2. Early announcements

They prevent a real or potential health risk, in order to alert the population and particularly vulnerable groups to being affected and minimize the threat of an infectious disease. Early announcements even when they lack all the necessary information avoid rumors and distorted information. The delay in disclosing the information will create the public's perception of an alarming situation and even more so if when it is disclosed it comes from an external (unofficial) source. The late announcements weaken the confidence of the population in the control of the epidemic outbreak by the health authorities.

3. Transparency

During a pandemic outbreak, achieving and maintaining public trust requires transparency, which implies providing timely and complete information about the actual or potential risk it represents and its control. It should be systematically updated to the public in the face of changes that occur. Transparency should characterize the relationship between managers, citizens and partners, contributing to a better collection of information, risk assessment and decision-making associated with the control of the epidemic outbreak.

4. Listen to the public.

To achieve effective communication in the management of emergency situations, it is essential to know the perception of risks, concerns and opinions of the public. Knowing how the public understands and perceives a certain risk, their beliefs and practices make it easier for them to make the right decisions and to influence the behavioral changes necessary to protect health.

5. Planning

Communication with the public during an outbreak is a major challenge for health authorities and requires rigorous planning that presupposes respect for the principles outlined above. Planning is an important principle that necessarily implies concrete action.

These guiding principles of communication for events of public health magnitude have traveled different paths, and today theoretical and methodological controversies persist that respond in one way or another to the actions of different states in the face of an event, sometimes unexpected, and in other cases such as a latent risk that finds the favorable conditions to become an epidemic outbreak, which requires the rapid intervention of the health system.

This chapter gives you **free tips on 7 essential rules** for effective risk communication, which are mentioned below:

1. Accept and involve the public as a legitimate partner.

2. Carefully plan and evaluate performance.

3. Listen to the public.

4. Be honest, frank and open.

5. Coordinate and collaborate with other credible sources.

6. Know the needs of the environment.

7. Speak clearly and compassionately.

From the perspective of the World Health Organization, various institutions have developed strategic communication guidelines to respond to these types of events, which require government commitment and will, and in them the ability of management of health systems, in order to preserve human lives and minimize material losses.

The characteristics of these events, their nature and repercussions contribute to the confluence of divergent views and approaches on the nature of communication and its actions from organizations to their audiences. Such is the case of the experience with the pandemic of influenza A (H1N1) - declared by the WHO, in June 2009, as the first of the 21st century -, basically supported by the risk communication standards, debated and approved by the WHO in 2005, those that respond to the needs of the environment; that is, of the general public, with special emphasis on risk groups.

In the analysis of the communication management process during the evolution of the pandemic, it is stated that said Organization was moving away from these principles and was approaching a crisis communication model (although it did not name it this way), changing the focus of his speech and focusing it on his defense. The communiqués became less regular and in some cases no information was disclosed to the public, despite the fact that it could be interpreted as a lack of transparency and decreased trust; two of the central values in the organization's communication strategy.

Although this experience marked a distancing in the last stages of communication management of the event, it suggested a review of the process by the agency to strengthen in practice the principles of risk communication that govern it and thus prepare for future events. It is also valid to estimate crisis communication, considering that the credibility of the information received by the public depends on the positive image of the organization.

Subsequent practices, such as those developed in the face of the Ebola virus epidemics in Africa and the Sika virus in South America and the Caribbean, have shown greater adherence to these principles, even with differential and perfectible communication management directions by different countries. They face situations of this nature, which has made it necessary to delimit the work of communication beyond its conceptualization and its leading role has been highlighted.

These practices will help to control the emergency with the least possible economic or social disturbance, since they give guidelines for the following actions:

• Act proactively with information and start communication with the public as soon as possible. Communicate to the different audiences what is known, what is unknown and the activities that are being carried out to obtain more information about the health situation.

• To guide the population affected by the emergency so that they can make decisions that allow them to protect their health, that of their family and that of their community.

• Disseminate information in a timely and transparent manner so as to establish and maintain public confidence in the authorities in charge of the emergency.

• Establish internal coordination mechanisms for the dissemination of information among scientists, technicians and authorities to establish a unique and coherent discourse that achieves public confidence, in addition to reducing fear and anxiety in it.

• Incorporate the community, addressing it using their own codes, depending on their interests and according to their knowledge and beliefs. In this way they will adopt healthy practices in the prevention and control of risk or disease.

• Establish a good relationship with the media and serve them regularly. It is important to keep the information according to the severity of the event.

• Address the population in a simple, transparent, frank and clear manner with guidelines and measures to face the impact on health.

• Show respect and empathy, recognize the fears and level of anxiety of the population.

• Identify and evaluate the contents of the information that will be disclosed to the public and decisions on the limits of what should be said and what is not necessary to report.

• Use diverse channels to converse with the public (surveys, online chats, call centers, among others).

• Follow up on the information disseminated in the media.

• Obtain the feedback of the messages based on the recommendations derived from the concerns of the population.

All this evolutionary process has allowed positive changes in communication, moving from a one-way communication to a two-way communication focused on the process, whose essential objective is to reach the population from their cultural references with an understandable language that mobilizes them to participate in the process. decision-making.

Risk communication as a process that establishes alliances and dialogues between authorities and citizens has continued to deepen and continues to develop today, as a result of the growing interest of the population in public health and safety, in understanding the risks to They may be exposed and have the right as citizens to participate in the stages of risk management and control.

In situations of public health emergencies, risk communication places citizen participation at the center of its actions, with an emphasis on groups of clinical risk and social vulnerability.

The participation of the population as a center of risk communication allows it to be actively integrated into the risk control process and help establish trust between institutions. It enables a greater global understanding of the process and decisions, and subsequently facilitates communication with the public about them. "

It will also promote knowledge and internalization of known and unknown risks, timely informing and sensitizing the public from planning about the needs and concerns to protect their health; For this, training and education actions will be developed to prevent and mitigate risk in different social areas such as: the family, the community, and labor and educational institutions.

All of the above confirms the decisive role of education and health promotion in risk prevention, always linked to participatory communication with a sociocultural approach, which should be specified in the risk communication strategy.

<u>The risk communication strategy as a key tool to face situations of public health emergencies.</u>

The risk communication strategy as a tool to face health emergency situations can be defined as "a dynamic and integrated work process that will allow the analysis of various possible scenarios, identify allies and collaborators, strengthen capacities, and establish monitoring mechanisms and process control, determine alternative communication channels such as mobile devices or others, as well as manage resources with the aim of minimizing the effects on human lives during the stages of an emergency or disaster in the shortest possible time. "

The implementation of the strategy will be in charge of a team trained to permanently coordinate the planned activities and their execution, so that efforts are optimized in the event of any event. An effective communication strategy must consider actions both in time of peace or normality and in time of emergency or disaster.

In fact, the communication strategy must start from a communication diagnosis that will allow the following elements to be identified:

- The organizations and social actors with which to coordinate the possible actions to be carried out.

- Information flows and communication mechanisms available between social actors and organizations.

- The material, technical and human resources available in the response team. The needs and degree of training of the health teams that may be involved.

-The perceptions of risk in the population associated with knowledge, myths and beliefs; and other cultural aspects anchored in the social imagination about disasters and how they can be controlled.

- The spaces and modes of social communication: places of circulation, confluence and meeting in the community, such as parks, schools, shopping areas, work centers, markets, social events, among others.

- The means of communication most used by the population, in all its formats, languages and scope (massive or community).

-The journalists, communicators and opinion leaders of relevance, specialized in emergencies or not, but who constitute authorized voices for their credibility in the public.

The results of the initial diagnosis will define how the communication strategy will be developed, which should consider the following steps:

1. Approach (it will be specified in what way the topic will be addressed, the theoretical and methodological framework in which the strategy will be sustained, the social groups that will be involved, the impact actions to be developed, among other aspects).

2. Objectives (they indicate the essence of what you want to achieve and they must be measurable, achievable, directed, reasonable, clear and specific).

3. Target audience (allows delimiting the content, the language to be used and selecting the channels and media to be used).

4. Content of the messages (select the topics of greatest interest to the public, the recommendations that are issued must correspond to the real possibilities of the population in order to be adopted).

5. Communication channels: print and electronic media, radio (educational radio spots, radio soap operas), television (educational spots, soap operas, documentaries), Internet (Internet conferences, blogs, social networks), alternative channels (talks in churches , telephone in the streets, radio amateur networks, among others).

6. Evaluation and feedback mechanisms (was the message received? Did the perception and behavior of the target group change? It involves the application of surveys, surveys, participatory evaluation workshops, among others).

After completing the steps for the initial diagnosis, the risk communication strategy will be designed, which will be developed in 5 stages: preparation, start of the emergency, control, recovery and evaluation.

In addition to the actions required in the strategy in relation to the preparation and evaluation stages, it is necessary to specify that after the onset of the emergency and the control stage, during the recovery phase, the actions focus on the dissemination of messages on hygiene and prevention, promoting community support and education for future emergencies.

The efficiency of a risk communication strategy for public health emergencies, supports its results in the education of the population and risk groups during the preparation stage, which will allow achieving important benefits, namely:

- Increase educational and preventive work in the population through health promotion, both for normal conditions and health crisis.

- Know the degree of knowledge of the population about a certain risk to identify the information needs existing in communities located in risk areas to communicate educational messages.

- Promote in the communities the appropriation and awareness of the information, so that its inhabitants identify their vulnerability and the alternatives they have to carry out preventive management.

- Take advantage of material and human resources in vulnerable communities in the face of a certain health risk, for the collective construction of preventive messages that respond to their socio-cultural characteristics and foster citizen participation from the preparation stage to the emergency recovery phase.

Health risk communication strategies will allow communication planning during all the stages of an emergency, having a proactive character and establishing control and monitoring of how information is received by the target audiences, to design new messages in the event that if necessary, in order to keep the public calm and attentive to the guidelines given at each stage of the emergency.

Without a doubt, the most important stage of the risk communication strategy is before the beginning of the health emergency; stage in which all the prevention work is carried out and the preparation to face a health risk in both normal and emergency situations.

These communication strategies should be considered open systems that are being refined in the face of new situations, because although there are health risks that can be triggered by known epidemiological events, there are others, such as disaster emergencies, where epidemics are widespread faster and more intense due to the complexity of the scenario in which they take place.

Risk communication as part of the institutional practices of health communication to face public health emergencies, should develop their parallel strategies to the implementation of health education strategies and health programs, in correspondence with the health risks to that the population in the different countries is exposed, with the communication policies established by these and the International Health Regulations approved by the WHO in situations of health emergency.

METHOD 2: HYGIENE PRACTICES

Every day, spoiled or contaminated food causes gastrointestinal diseases in hundreds of people in our country, additionally thousands of tons of food are wasted due to mishandling and poor storage.

The deterioration and contamination of the products are mainly caused by bacteria, microscopic organisms capable of producing toxins and causing illness in people who consume the affected food.

It should be noted that many times the contaminated products do not show apparent changes, so that consumers cannot see the risk they pose to their health.

Considering the above, it highlights the importance of preventing food contamination through the application of good hygiene and sanitation practices (BPHS).

BPHS are a series of activities and procedures that prevent the risks of contamination and deterioration of products, as well as eliminate bacteria capable of causing disease which if care is not taken can lead to a pandemic, a war of life and death.

Good hygiene practices are those where specific cleaning procedures must be followed before, during and after carrying out some type of work with the final objective of minimizing the microbial risk in products for personal consumption.

What are good hygiene practices?

Any person who comes into contact with raw materials, ingredients, packaging material, products in process and finished, equipment and utensils, must perform some of the following hygiene practices:

- Wearing clean clothing appropriate to the type of work performed, including footwear, must be kept clean and in good condition, in addition to not wearing it outside the plant.
- Wash hands and clean them before starting work, after each absence from work and at any time during the day when they may be dirty or contaminated. Operators should wash their hands thoroughly, from the middle of the forearm to the tips of the fingers, with soap and scrubbing with energy, using a nail brush and fingertips; After rinsing, soak hands in sanitizing solution, dry in air dryer or with disposable paper towel. Cloth towels should never be used.
- Keep nails short, clean and free from paint and enamel.
- Wear a mouthpiece, ensuring that the nose and mouth are covered.
- Avoid any contamination with expectorations, mucus, cosmetics, hair, chemical substances, medications or any other foreign material.

- Hair should be kept clean, wear protection that completely covers the hair, and wear it on the plant at all times.
- Beard and facial hair are not allowed, unless they are fully protected.
- Smoking, chewing, eating or drinking can only be done in pre-established areas, where the risk of contamination is minimal.
- Dispense with pens, pens, thermometers, glasses, tools, pins, bras, or other removable objects in the top pockets of clothing.
- No jewelry or ornaments should be worn: hair clips, barrettes, clips, earrings, rings, bracelets and watches, necklaces or others that may contaminate the product, even when worn under a protection.
- If cut or wounded, they should be covered appropriately with a sanitary material (gauze, bandages) and put on some waterproof material (plastic finger, plastic glove), before entering the process area.

Good hygiene practices are mainly used in the following industries:

- Food
- Cosmetics
- Medical
- Pharmaceutical
- Suppliers of safety products

METHOD 3: SOCIAL DISTANCING

The World Health Organization (WHO) recommends establishing public health measures as practice partner distancing l to combat pandemics . Social distancing are the measures taken to stop or stop the spread of a contagious disease . In the case of an individual, it refers to maintaining a sufficient distance between him and another person to reduce the risk of inhaling the drops that are produced when an infected person coughs or sneezes . In a community, measures of social distancing can include limiting or canceling large gatherings of people , explains the Harvard Medical School .

These measures are also aimed at young people , who although most will pass the disease with mild symptoms, could infect people at risk as we already explained here .

Social distancing means, according to the CDC (the Centers for Disease Control and Prevention of the United States) , not entering places where close contact with many other people can occur (shopping malls, cinemas, stadiums), avoiding crowds of people and keep distance (about 2 meters) with other people if possible .

As we already explained , this seeks to flatten the epidemic curve and that the health system can absorb all cases .

With influenza A and the Spanish influenza these measures reduced transmission.

These measures have shown their effectiveness in the past. A study on the closings of schools , cinemas and restaurants for 18 days and other measures of social distance in Mexico during the influenza A pandemic in 2009 associated it with a reduction of between 29% and 37% in the transmission rate of a flu. Another historical example. In 1918, at the start of the pandemic known as the Spanish flu , two American cities took social distancing measures differently.

While in Philadelphia, Pennsylvania, the first cases were reported on September 17, authorities allowed large public gatherings, including a large parade on September 28. It was not until October 3 (16 days later) that social distancing was implemented, when the health system was already overwhelmed.

On the other hand, in San Luis (Missouri) on October 5, the first cases of Spanish influenza were reported. Two days later, the authorities took measures of social distancing .

Philadelphia had a considerably larger epidemic, with a maximum of 257 deaths per 100,000 inhabitants compared to 31 in San Luis while social distancing measures were being applied. In total, in Philadelphia that fall there was an excess of 719 deaths per 100,000 inhabitants compared to the usual, while in San Luis the rate was only 347 deaths per 100,000 inhabitants, less than half .

According to a study that analyzed measures taken by 17 US cities during the 1918 pandemic, cities that took various measures of social distancing early in the pandemic had a peak death rate around 50% lower than those cities that did not implement them and had a less pronounced epidemic curve . The accumulated excess mortality was around 20% less in the cities that did take early measures since these decisions did not last more than 6 weeks.

No intervention alone was associated with a general reduction in deaths, but it was associated with multiple measures of social distancing. This supports the hypothesis that taking these social distance measures quickly can significantly reduce influenza transmission, but viral spread increases when the measures are relaxed, according to the study authors.

Measures You Can Take To Increase Social Distancing

- Here are 15 measures of social distancing to reduce the expansion a pandemic:
    - Stay home as much as possible , limit contact with people when you are out and avoid crowded spaces.
    - Avoid hugging or kissing or shaking hands when greeting people who don't live with you or who do but who have gone out and haven't washed their hands yet.

- Avoid meetings where the space between people is less than one meter .
- Avoid eating in restaurants, going to crowded bars , attending religious services, and traveling on public transportation during peak hours.
- Wash your hands after you are out of the house and before touching the places in your house.
- Hand towels should be washed clean every time, in other words, you can use a disposable paper
- Try not to touch your face .
- Telecommute as much as possible .
- Use large meeting rooms for face-to-face meetings , sit more than a meter away, don't shake hands.
- Avoid unnecessary travel .
- Avoid socializing in small spaces where people are closer than a meter.
- Avoid eating in crowded dining rooms or restaurants, take your lunch to work .
- If you use public transport or shared computers, carry disinfectant wipes and clean the surfaces you are going to touch .
- Use a hand sanitizer after touching a shared surface, or wash your hands thoroughly with soap and water after touching a shared surface.
- If you handle money or customer payments , use hand sanitizer frequently and avoid touching your face .

Conclusion

Both Risk communication, maintaining good hygiene and social distancing, as a systematic practice in the public health system will strengthen the prevention and health education work in the population, with an emphasis on clinical risk groups and vulnerable communities, which will allow avoiding or mitigating material and human losses. in situations of public health emergency. For the effective implementation of the risk communication strategy, as a key tool to face situations of public health emergency, it must be supported by the theoretical foundations of risk communication, in the health emergency experiences led by the WHO in the framework of the International Health Regulations and in the health and communication policies established by each country.

CHAPTER FIVE:

ECONOMIC PANDEMIC

An event as tragic and unexpected as the rapid contagion of thousands of people around the world (and, unfortunately, the death of many, terrible!) Is causing our economies to falter. Events unfold so quickly that the numbers of those affected are changing hour by hour. WHO has already announced that we are facing a pandemic. Without prior immunization, vaccines or retroviral, for the moment, our only form of prevention is a lot of hygiene, and even more responsibility to avoid infections.

Since the end of last year, governments have been closely following developments in the Wuhan Coronavirus, concerned about the effects on populations

Due to the situation facing the world, have implemented measures to prevent infection and protect the health of its inhabitants. However, epidemics also have negative effects on economies. First, it is costly to establish virus containment plans and care for the infected population. So when there is a case of contagion in a country, economic imbalances arise both from the effects of containment plans and from the fear of contagion.

So, we are led to ask ourselves: **What is the impact of pandemic on the world economy?**

Increased transmission of the virus can weaken consumer demand and harm tourism, commerce and the service sector in affected countries.

The first thing we have to understand is the difference between: Endemic, epidemic and pandemic.

Endemic: when a disease occurs periodically in a specific region. Ex: Malaria.

Epidemic: There is a very rapid and unexpected increase in infections over a period of time in a specific region. Ex: SARS.

Pandemic: it is an epidemic that becomes international and there is an unexpected increase around the world. In addition, the infections begin to occur locally and not only from where the disease originates. Ex: H1N1.

The main economic imbalances in the countries arise from the new needs of the health systems, possible closings of companies, shops, and educational centers. In general, there is a significant reduction in the productivity of a country or region. The economic consequences are not the same for all countries, as some have better health systems and more or less robust economies.

Cost of diseases worldwide

2003	SARS	$ 40,000 million
2009	H1N1	$ 50,000 million
2013	Ebola	$ 53,000 million
2020	Wuhan coronavirus	$ 280 000 Million (est)

Some economic implications of the main diseases worldwide

Acute and Severe Respiratory Syndrome (SARS)

It is a highly contagious respiratory disease, caused by the Coronavirus. It first appeared in Asia in February 2003, rapidly affecting more than 20 countries in North America, South America, and Europe.

According to data from the World Health Organization (WHO), worldwide there were 8,098 people infected, of whom 774 died from the disease.

The impact of this virus represented a contraction of world GDP by 0.1% during 2003. According to the newspaper El País, the global costs of this epidemic in that period was $ 40 billion.

Asian countries were the most affected economically, mainly affecting tourism, hotels and transportation.

H1N1 virus

Also known as "swine fever" or "influenza," it first appeared in the United States in 2009, but it became a pandemic as it spread rapidly around the world.

This virus contained a unique combination of influenza virus genes that had never before been identified in humans or animals. Preliminary figures from the WHO in 2009 indicated that the deaths from this virus reached 18,641, however, the exact number is unknown and it is feared that it will be up to 10 times higher.

Although the virus appeared in North America, the economy of the southern cone of the American continent was most affected by H1N1. Economic losses in 2009 are estimated to have ranged from 0.5% to 1.5% of GDP in affected countries.

US $ 50 Billion: Global costs of the H1N1 virus in the world for 2009

Ebola

In 2014 there was an Ebola epidemic on the African continent, specifically in Nigeria, Mali, Senegal, the Democratic Republic of the Congo, Sierra Leone, Liberia and Guinea. These last three countries were the most affected, since there were 28 610 infected people and 11,308 deaths between 2014 and 2016. In this same period there were also infections in the United States, Spain, the United Kingdom and Italy.

To combat the effects of this epidemic, the infected countries contemplated strategies to respond to both the humanitarian crisis and the economic crisis. The recovery cost for Liberia, Sierra Leone, and Guinea is estimated to be $ 812 million, $ 844 million, and $ 2.89 billion, respectively.

US $ 53,000 million: Global economic losses of Ebola during 2014.

Wuhan coronavirus (2019-2020)

This virus is considered as the most damaging in the economic field, since China is a world power and the effects on its economy have global repercussions. In the first months of the year, the Chinese economy could be affected by up to 2% of GDP . This has had an impact on oil demand, as China is the world's largest importer. Even the low productivity in the country has affected companies whose factories are located in China.

Finally, the World Bank lowered the forecasts for global economic growth for the first half of 2020, from 5.5% to 5.4%.

US $ 280,000 million: Possible final costs of the Wuhan Coronavirus worldwide.

The unexpected economic effects of coronavirus

It is very likely that the screen of this computer, the phone of your cell phone or the tablet that you are reading this has been made in China or at least uses components made there. Other equally affected sectors around the world are:

Textile industry: The main affectation of the sector has been due to the closings of factories, due to the prevention due to the agglomeration of people. For example in Suzhou (China Town) 80% of wedding dresses are produced that are sold worldwide. The main buyer of Chinese textiles is the United States.

Cell Phone Shortage - Technology Industry: China is the world's largest manufacturer and exporter of cell phones. Apple announced on February 17 that the global supply of IPhone will be affected due to the outbreak of the disease. Furthermore, there has been a 50% drop in China's smartphone exports (October 2019 to March 2020).

Air transport: The International Air Transport Association (IATA) said on February 21 that airlines will lose $ 29.3 billion in 2020 due to the coronavirus outbreak.

Oil consumption : The consumption of this worldwide has fallen since the beginning of the year, this because China is the main consumer of oil in the world. A drop of more than 20% is reported after the coronavirus outbreak.

Industrial and manufacturing sector: The closure of major factories in Italy (a country heavily affected by the coronavirus) could severely affect the production of European cars. In the case of China, industrial machinery is also considered an important export product.

World

According to the Observatory of Economic Complexity (OEC), China is the world's largest exporter, with sales of close to $ 2.2 trillion in 2019.

China's main export sectors are:

- Machinery and electrical equipment (26%)
- Machinery including computers (17.2%)
- Furniture, lights, signs, prefabricated buildings (3.9%)
- Plastic and plastic items (3.2%)
- Vehicles (3%)

In Latin America, the countries most exposed to the effects of the coronavirus with Chile and Peru. The reason: Chilean exports to China represent 33% of its total and the figure is 25% for the Peruvian case. For Brazil and Argentina it is less than 15% in each one.

Since 2005, China has provided loans worth more than $ 140 billion in Latin America, almost as much as it has in Africa. The country has also invested, with the participation of Chinese companies in private and public projects. The repercussions in China will undoubtedly be reflected in South America.

Central America

Since 2012, China has become the second best trading partner in the region, replacing a significant part of imports from the United States. Chinese imports to Central America have grown at a rate of 13.1% (ECLAC 2018).

According to the Secretariat of Central American Economic Integration (SIECA), the pa í ses Central imported goods from China for $ 8.922 million in 2018.

It has been proven that the world economy suffers from the great epidemics of the world. The economic effects are more evident in countries with higher cases of infection. Notwithstanding the foregoing, when these countries are world powers, economic imbalances become global.

The Chinese economy is so relevant that it is affecting the rest of the world economies. In fact, China's economy could be affected by up to 2% of GDP. Due to the economic impact, some experts claim to be in the presence of an economic pandemic.

The coronavirus that emerged in China is the most pressing uncertainty facing the global economy and a threat to the fragile global recovery.

Centuries ago, ships were required to quarantine ports during pests to prevent their spread to coastal cities. Flights from Italy to Spain or to the United States from Europe are now prohibited. Pandemic can devastate the world in several waves resulting to a rise in economic collapse, especially between the fourteenth and eighteenth centuries, ending the lives of some 100 million people in Europe, Africa and Asia (between 25 and 60 % of the European population, according to estimates).

Consequences Of Other Epidemics

Another epidemic that sank the economy was the 1918 flu (badly called the "Spanish" flu as it was one of the first countries where it was reported, as it was foreign to the war), which caused more deaths than World War I (some 50 million according to estimates). Between illness and strife economic activity sank and there were changes in migratory movements, although it is difficult to discern how much of the collapse of the economy can be attributed to each phenomenon.

More recent infectious outbreaks, including fears of some relatively contained ones, have affected trade in recent decades. For example, the European Union's ban on exporting British beef lasted for ten years due to an outbreak of mad cow disease in the UK, although transmission to humans is relatively limited

Furthermore, some protracted epidemics, such as HIV and malaria, discourage foreign direct investment. An International Monetary Fund report on epidemics estimates the expected annual cost of pandemic flu at about $ 500 billion (0.6% of global income), including lost income and the intrinsic cost of increased mortality.

And although the health effect of an outbreak is relatively limited, its economic consequences can multiply rapidly. For example, Liberia saw its GDP growth decline of 8 percentage points between 2013 and 2014 during the Ebola outbreak in West Africa despite the country's overall low death rate during that period

Winners And Losers In Epidemics

The effects of outbreaks and epidemics are not equitably distributed in the economy. Some sectors could even benefit financially, while others will suffer excessively. Pharmacists who produce vaccines, antibiotics, or other products necessary for the outbreak response are potential beneficiaries. In all situations there are economic sectors that benefit.

When there is an exceptional demand for certain goods and services, the sectors that provide them "make their August" (it could be the case of masks or staple foods these days), while those that provide goods and services that we leave behind sink. to consume and those that are affected by the interruption of components and raw materials

But inequality is also reflected in disease and mortality. Right now, one of the great causes of inequality in the impact of an epidemic is access to medical care. In countries that lack public universal health care systems, where diagnostic tests, treatments, and hospitalization have to be paid for (the US case), the level of income will be decisive

Literature As A Historical Source On Pandemics

The teacher remembers three literary works that are highly valuable historical sources on epidemics: Boccaccio's Decameron describes the plague that struck Florence in 1348; the Diary of the Plague Year, written by Daniel Defoe in 1722, which recounts the plague epidemic that London suffered in 1665, which killed a fifth of the population.

"All three tell us about fear, about how society faces massive and unexpected death, some looking for guilty parties and accusing certain groups or individuals, resorting to magic and religion ... others trying to understand the scientific causes of what happens, looking for rational and civic solutions that advance society and alleviate the adverse economic effects of these crises.

Summary

What is the impact of pandemic on the world economy? Since the end of last year, governments have been closely following developments in the Wuhan Coronavirus, concerned about the effects on the world's populations and economy.

With the current advance of the disease, already classified as a pandemic, final costs of US $ 280 billion are estimated worldwide.

CHAPTER SIX:

VACCINES: A PREVENTIVE MEASURE AGAINST PANDEMIC?

Vaccines are a preventive treatment that strengthens the immune system to prevent potentially serious or life-threatening infectious diseases, in some cases.

Vaccines consist of biological products that prevent infectious diseases by activating our immune system so that it develops antibodies against these diseases.

Vaccines "teach" the body to defend itself against viruses and bacteria . This is possible because a small amount of the infectious agent, dead or dormant germ (attenuated vaccine) is inoculated when a vaccine is given, allowing the immune system to recognize it. It is then that the antibodies neutralize the causative agents of the disease and prevent it from developing.

They also provide immunity to future encounters with the microorganism, so that an immune response to infection will be more easily triggered in the future.

Some vaccines are given in the first days of life but the vast majority start after two months . The baby's immune system is capable of receiving many vaccines at once; Babies have a great capacity to generate an immune response.

Types of vaccines

- Some vaccines are single dose and others need a booster or multiple doses.
- Live attenuated virus vaccines: Viruses are very weakened, so they do not cause disease, they only generate immunity. An example is MMR or chickenpox vaccine.
- Inactivated microorganism vaccines: a part (protein) of the virus or bacteria is inoculated. An example is the flu shot

- Toxoid vaccines: the toxin that causes the virus or bacteria is used, making us immune to the harmful effects of the infection and not to the infection itself. An example, tetanus or diphtheria.
- Biosynthetic vaccines: Artificial substances similar to pieces of infectious agents are inoculated. An example is the Haemphilus Influenzae type B (Hib) conjugate vaccine.

Vaccination schedule

The vaccination schedule is the chronological sequence of vaccines that are routinely administered in a country or geographic area and whose purpose is to obtain adequate immunization in the population against diseases for which an effective vaccine is available. Each year pediatric societies prepare a calendar with the recommended vaccines for the coming year. It is a way to carry out an exhaustive review of preventive strategies in the child population.

Vaccines in the vaccination calendar are divided into:

- Systematic vaccinations for all children
- Hepatitis B
- Diphtheria
- Tetanus
- Whooping cough
- Polio
- Haemophilus influenzae type b bacteria
- Meningococcus C
- Pneumococcus
- Measles
- Rubella
- Mumps
- Human papilloma virus (for girls).
- Recommended immunizations and at the family's choice
- Rotavirus

- Meningococcus B (infants)
- Chickenpox (children)
- Vaccines for risk groups

They are indicated for children suffering from a serious or chronic disease. This section includes the influenza vaccine and the hepatitis A vaccine.

Negative Beliefs About Vaccination

Vaccines are an essential instrument for the prevention of infectious diseases. However, false ideas and unsubstantiated rumors about possible negative effects can discourage vaccination, with consequent risks for the protection of the population. One of the reason for this chapter is to evaluate the origin and arguments of some of the most frequent errors and rumors about eventual adverse effects of vaccinations. Vaccines, like any drug, can cause adverse effects, but the eventual adverse effects of vaccination programs are clearly inferior to their individual benefits (to the vaccinated) and collective (to the vaccinated and to those who cannot be vaccinated for medical reasons). Any undesirable effects attributable to vaccines must be detectable by powerful and well-structured pharmacovigilance systems.

However, false ideas and rumors with no scientific foundation about their possible negative effects may dissuade people from being vaccinated, with the consequent risks for the health of the population. The objective of this chapter is to evaluate the origin and the arguments of some of the most frequent mistaken ideas and rumors about the possible adverse effects of vaccines. However, as disease, disability and death from immuno-preventable diseases have declined - thanks in particular to the impact of vaccination programs - concern about vaccine safety has increased, by contrast. Although a person is much more likely to be affected by an immune preventable disease than by the effect of a vaccine, some people choose not to get vaccinated or not vaccinate their children with the recommended vaccines due to inadequate perceptions of the risk of illness or safety vaccine .

Certainly the history of vaccines shows adverse events related to vaccine safety; some have been confirmed and the vast majority, based on initial suspicions or associations, have been ruled out after the investigations carried out. A first example is the "Cutter Incident", which occurred in 1955 3months after Jonas Salk discovered the first inactivated polio vaccine and the first mass vaccination program against polio began in the United States. Poliomyelitis was at that time a serious public health problem due to the epidemics it produced, coming to be considered as the second concern for Americans after the atomic bomb. Some batches of the vaccine were poorly manufactured and contained live viruses instead of the inactivated viruses described in the Salk protocol. Despite having passed the required safety tests, there were more than 40,000 polio cases, 250 cases of paralytic polio, and 10 deaths attributed to vaccines produced in a family business (Cutter Laboratories), while vaccines manufactured by other laboratories were not. caused problems. The vaccine was withdrawn after detection of the first cases of polio. This incident was decisive in the history of vaccine manufacturing, as substantial modifications were established in government supervision of vaccines with strict rules on protocols, improvement of manufacturing safety systems, and development of epidemiological surveillance. Following these corrections, vaccination against polio was resumed. Then, it was obvious that myths and wrong perceptions and beliefs as regards vaccines are definitely false.

Hesitancy Vaccine: Adapted Answers

Hesitation about vaccines is a complex and multifaceted phenomenon. Its approach must also take into account the diversity of the audiences concerned.

Critical reactions and attitudes have been noted since the onset of vaccination. Thus, in 1850 already, a League opposed to vaccination against smallpox was created in the United Kingdom. The arguments of opponents of vaccination are well known and are mainly based on 3 statements (and their specific versions): vaccination causes more damage than disease; the vaccine contains toxic constituents;

vaccination does not give lasting immunity.

But the phenomenon called in Anglo-Saxon literature " vaccine hesitancy " is far from being limited to the only opposition to vaccination.

The Strategic Advisory Group of Experts (SAGE) convened by WHO defines it as follows: "By hesitation with regard to vaccines, we mean the delay in accepting or refusing vaccines despite the availability of services vaccination. It is a complex phenomenon, specific to the context and varying according to the time, place and vaccines. It includes certain factors such as the underestimation of danger, convenience and confidence.

Acceptance of vaccination is generally the norm in the Belgian and European population. However, a limited proportion of people accept certain vaccines while hesitating on the merits of their decision and / or delay the timing of vaccination compared to recommended schedules and / or refuse certain vaccines or the vaccination as a whole.

In reality, there is a gradient of hesitation attitudes between the two extremes, made up on the one hand by people fully adhering to the vaccination programs offered by the health authorities and on the other hand by the opponents of any vaccination.

Experts therefore consider that vaccination coverage rates are not a reliable reflection of the phenomenon of hesitation with regard to vaccines.

Determinants of hesitation about vaccines

Acceptance of vaccination is considered a complex behavioral phenomenon that results from a decision-making process influenced by multiple factors.

A working group set up by WHO in 2011 proposed a model based on 3 categories : the elements linked to the underestimation of the danger, those linked to the convenience of vaccination and those linked to confidence.

The underestimation of the danger is present when the risks of vaccine-preventable disease are perceived as low and vaccination is not considered as a necessary preventive action.

It is influenced by many factors, including the competition between life or health priorities at a given time in life.

The success of vaccination programs feeds it, paradoxically, by contributing to an apparent disappearance of the threat linked to an infectious disease

the trust encompasses aspects such as belief in the efficacy and safety of the vaccine, the quality of the vaccination program (including the reliability and competence of the health services), transparency of political motivations and decision-making processes. the convenience of immunization covers such things as:

- Availability of the vaccination offer,
- Economic and geographic accessibility,an ability to understand the offer (language and health literacy), etc.

Convenience also covers the feeling (perceived and / or real quality) of the relationship with the health system and the correlation of the organization of the latter (places, times, etc.) with the context of life and the expectations of populations (comfort, respect for cultural diversity, etc.).

With reference to this model, the working group has drawn up a list of determinants of hesitation with regard to vaccines, reproduced below.

Determinants of hesitation about vaccines

Influences of the context: Influences linked to history, socio-cultural factors, the environment, the health system, economic and political factors.

- Communication and media environment
- Opinion leaders, promoter of the vaccination program and pro and anti-vaccination lobbies
- Historical influences
- Religion, culture, gender, socio-economic factors
- Policies
- Geographic barriers
- Perception of the pharmaceutical industry

Individual and group influences: Influences related to the personal perception of the vaccine or influences of the social environment and peers.

- Personal, family and / or community members' experience with immunization (pain included)
- Beliefs and attitudes towards health and prevention
- Knowledge and awareness
- Confidence and personal experience in the healthcare system and providers
- Perception of the risk / benefit ratio
- Vaccination perceived as social norm versus useless or harmful

Factors specific to a vaccine or vaccination

- Risk / benefit ratio in terms of epidemiology and scientific evidence
- Introduction of a new vaccine or formulation or recommendation for an existing vaccine
- Administration mode
- Organization of the vaccination program / mode of administration (routine or mass campaign)
- Reliability and source of supply of vaccines and / or vaccination equipment
- Vaccination schedules
- Costs

- Strength of recommendation and / or knowledge base and / or attitudes of health professionals

We note that the determinants of hesitation with regard to vaccines, such as education or socioeconomic status, do not act unequivocally (contrary to what is observed for the social determinants of health). Indeed, a high level of education can just as well be associated with a low or high acceptance of vaccination. This is further confirmed by the reluctance towards vaccination felt by some doctors.

Communication can negatively influence the use of immunization when it is poor or inadequate.

Based on this modeling, WHO and UNICEF have included questions about reluctance about vaccines in their annual information collections from national immunization program managers. In 2013, 68% of countries answered one of the questions asked "What are the 3 main reasons for not accepting vaccines from the national program" . The 3 reasons most often reported were: beliefs, attitudes and motivation towards health and prevention, the risk / benefit ratio of vaccines and the environment of communication and media information.

Stakes

According to the European office of the WHO, it is essential to preserve the achievements, in terms of public health, of the vaccination programs put in place for decades.

The impact of these programs is dependent on the availability and quality of vaccines and immunization services, as well as on the conviction and commitment of health professionals and decision-makers. But it is also based on the just perception by populations of concepts such as:

- the benefits and risks of vaccination,

- the existence of preventable infectious diseases and the risks of complications that accompany them
- the decision-making and vaccine recommendation process
- parental responsibilities for protecting children from preventable diseases.
- Strategies implemented in response to reluctance regarding vaccines
- Responding to hesitation about vaccines is not an easy task, given the multitude of elements that can potentially influence an individual's decision-making process, whether for their own vaccination or for their own child.

The main pitfall to keep in mind is precisely that there is no single factor, nor a homogeneous population of hesitant people , this implies for authorities (at the level of a country, of a region), to finance studies and analyzes based on modeling in 3 categories (underestimation of the danger, convenience of vaccination and confidence) which will allow better understand the phenomenon (eg geographic, cultural, religious, socio-economic aspects, etc.). Thanks to the consideration of this complexity, interventions adapted to different subgroups, contexts, vaccines, etc. can be built for individual vaccinators , to listen to their patients, to analyze the reasons for their hesitations. By favoring a benevolent attitude of non-judgment, they can then develop information and advice adapted to the characteristics of each type of patient.

Following this reasoning, on the initiative of the European Technical Advisory Group of Experts on Immunization , a guide was proposed in 2013: Guide to tailoring immunization programs .

A systematic review of the peer reviewed and gray literature (from January 2007 to October 2013) made it possible to identify the strategies usually used to respond to the problems posed by hesitation with regard to vaccines . Among the latter, few have been evaluated in terms of either impact on vaccination rates, or in terms of changes in knowledge, attitudes or behavior. These strategies most often focused on influenza, the human papillomavirus and vaccination of children in the geographical area of the Americas. The majority of actions were aimed at increasing knowledge and awareness.

Only thirteen studies (out of more than 170) could be considered for establishing grade evidence. There was moderate quality evidence in favor of: the use of social mobilization, mass media, training tools for health professionals; non-financial incentives; sending reminders. In general, interventions with multiple approaches and based on dialogue were more effective.

It appears, however, on the basis of this literature review, that the approaches developed and published so far do not take sufficient account of the multiplicity of determinants of hesitation with regard to vaccines, nor of the heterogeneity of the sub -groups of populations concerned.

In addition, there is often a great temptation for vaccine policy-makers to use simple information or social marketing as the main response to hesitation about vaccines.

The limits of social marketing

Social marketing is too often presented as a miracle solution to respond to hesitations about vaccination, when it is only one of the avenues to be exploited.

The social marketing approach has specificities that must be understood to understand the constraints and limits of its use. Unlike commercial marketing, which targets the sale of products and is content to adapt to the wishes of the consumer, social marketing seeks the well-being of the public by questioning or even shaking up certain public wishes. In addition to the immediate gratification sought by marketing (the purchase of the desired object), social marketing offers a far superior product in the long term (the absence of a hypothetical infection occurring in the future for vaccination).

More fundamentally, commercial marketing does not seek to change the consumer, whereas social marketing wants to modify attitudes, values, behaviors; the challenge is to give "meaning", in everyone's eyes, to the practice of vaccination.

In addition, social marketing put at the service of health cannot be satisfied with a search for efficiency. There are ethical limits: the end, however honorable it may be, does not justify all means (for example blunt propaganda in favor of vaccination)

Now, let's move to trypanophobia, the fear of injection, and how to overcome so as to be able to be injected without having fear, in order to be immune to diseases.

Fear of injections (trypanophobia): causes, symptoms, and consequences

Extreme and irrational fear of injections is one of the most common and feared phobias.

One of the most frequent extreme fears, which is not only present in children, is injection phobia or trypanophobia .

Trypanophobes have a really bad time when they have to give themselves an injection and go to the health center. And, in many cases, they can even avoid these situations without caring about putting their lives at risk (by not getting vaccinated against diseases like tetanus) or reducing pain or inflammation with corticosteroids.

This phobia is one of the most common, calculating that about 10% of the population suffers from it to some degree. Sometimes trypanophobia can be confused with fear of blood (hematophobia) or fear of sharp objects (aicmophobia) ; however, fear of injections can only be a great fear of these objects. Some specific phobic stimuli are spiders, snakes, lifts, or flying.

Other types of phobias

In addition to this group of phobias, which are also known as simple phobias, there are two more that are social phobias , involving other people or social situations such as performance anxiety, fear of shame or humiliation or appreciation.

Causes of trypanophobia

The fear of injections usually develops during childhood and in many cases tends to last into adulthood. Its cause is often a traumatic experience in childhood or adolescence, and although the injections do not really cause much pain, these people interpret it as a serious threat to their physical integrity. It is not that they think they are going to die from the injection, but that the pain will be so strong that they will not be able to bear it.

Learning this fear often occurs through what is known as classical conditioning , a type of associative learning that Ivan Pávlov, a Russian physiologist, initially investigated, but made famous by the behaviorist John B. Watson , who believed that human beings could learn strong conditioning emotions and then generalize them to similar situations.

For this he devised a series of experiments with children, and in one of them he managed to make a small boy named Albert learn to be afraid of a white rat that he adored at first. This experiment could not be carried out today because it is considered unethical. You can see it in the video below:

Other causes of this phobia

This phobia can often develop by vicarious conditioning , that is, by observation. For example, in the case that a child sees an adult who panics when giving an injection, or for watching a movie that shows injections or syringes.

Some theorists also think that the causes may be genetic; and others who are predisposed to suffer certain phobias. In this sense, phobic disorders are formed by primitive and non-cognitive associations , which are not easily modifiable by logical arguments.

Symptoms of fear of injections

Fear of injections presents the same symptoms as any phobia, where there is a predominance of anxiety and discomfort and an exaggerated attempt to avoid situations in which the phobic stimulus may appear.

The symptoms of trypanophobia are:

• Cognitive symptoms : fear and anxiety in front of syringes and the possibility of receiving an injection, anguish, confusion, lack of concentration, irrational thoughts ...

• Behavioral symptoms : avoidance of any situation in which the person may receive an injection.

• Physical symptoms : acceleration of the pulse, hyperventilation, stomach pain and nausea, feeling of suffocation, dry mouth, etc.

Conclusion

There are different currents that can be useful to treat trypanophobia; however, cognitive behavioral therapy seems to provide the best results. This type of therapy aims to modify internal events (thoughts, emotions, beliefs, etc.) and behaviors that are considered to be causing the discomfort.

Therefore, different techniques are used, among which the relaxation techniques (especially indicated for specific moments in which the person experiences great anxiety) and the systematic desensitization , which is a type of exposure technique in which, as its name indicates, the patient is gradually exposed to phobic stimulation.

To treat this phobia, it is also possible to use cognitive therapy based on Mindfulness or acceptance and commitment therapy , both of which belong to third-generation therapies, and do not intend to modify behaviors but rather accept the experience, which automatically reduces symptoms because there is no resistance to the facts. In specific and extreme cases, anxiolytics can be administered; however, always with psychotherapy.

CHAPTER SEVEN:

CORONAVIRUS: ALL YOU NEED TO KNOW

Since the latest epidemic turned pandemic is the novel COVID 19, I have decided to make this chapter a bonus for all my dear readers, giving you all the nooks and crannies that surrounds the deadly disease, affecting the world, economy and lives. After this chapter, you will also read about the effect of corona virus on mental and psychological health of human, giving vivid explanations, citations and result as well, flip through!.

Brief Historical Concepts: the General things you need to know about Coronavirus

The Coronavirus was first discovered in the 1960s. The coronavirus has evolved a lot since this time.

In 2002, a virus known as SARS coronavirus emerged in humans. This disease likely jumped from an animal reservoir to humans. The SARS was believed to have been transferred from horseshoe bats.

The 2002 SARS coronavirus also originated from Guangdong province in China and this disease caused atypical pneumonia capable of being fatal if not promptly treated.

The disease spread from China to Hong Kong and quickly spread to almost all parts of Europe, North America and Asia. The spread was more in East Asia and some parts of Europe.

By the end of May 2003, over 8,000 cases were confirmed, and this disease caused more than 800 deaths. Strict measures and prohibitions ensured, and this disease was finally curtailed by and around June 2003. Prohibitions and restrictions gradually got lifted, and the spread slowly came to a halt around the end of 2003. The SARS of 2002 was a zoonotic disease. Zoonotic diseases are disease capable of jumping from animal hosts (reservoir) to humans. Such disease includes but not limited to infections like Ebola, SARS and Lassa Fever.

The SARS coronavirus of 2002 caused panic, and the major mode of transmission then was through droplets from sneezing, cough and other bodily fluids.

Intro to Coronavirus:

Coronavirus is a collective name given to any virus which belongs to the family 'Coronaviridae'.
The virus has enveloped virions with an approximate measurement of 120nm – 400nm in diameter.

The word CORONA means Crown. The shape of a coronavirus is club-shaped glycoprotein spikes which give it a crownlike shape. The coronavirus has a coronal appearance, and from this, the name was derived "Coronavirus".

The coronavirus (coronaviridae) genome consists of a single strand of positive-sense Ribonucleic acid (RNA). The capsid is helical or tubular.

This coronaviridae generally has two genera. The genera consist of Coronavirus and Torovirus, and both differ in nucleocapsid morphology. Coronavirus is more helical, but Torovirus is more tubular.

The coronavirus is a very active agent involved in gastrointestinal diseases found in poultry, bovine and humans.

For example, in humans, the SARS coronavirus causes severe acute respiratory syndromes.

The new coronavirus jumped from animal to human, and this shows an undoubtedly required genetic mutation. For this virus to jump from animals to humans, it means it achieved the required genetic changes.

Presently, the SARS virus found in Horsehoe bats are not able to infect humans directly, but the novel coronavirus infects humans directly. This change of genetic mechanism might have possibly occurred in the Palm civet.

In 2012, another form of Coronavirus called the MERS (Middle East Respiratory Syndrome was also discovered in human subjects, and this was first found in Saudi Arabia. The following year, 2013, other infections were reported in Jordan, Qatar, Germany, France and other countries. All these cases have a direct or indirect link to the Middle East.

For the MERS of 2012; all cases reported from 2012 to 2019 shows roughly one-third of the infected people ended up dying from the disease.

MERS passes from bats to other animals and then from these animals gets transmitted to humans. The possible reservoir of MERS virus is Camel.

In October 2019. A virus directly related to SARS or MERS of (2002 and 2012) emerged in Wuhan city, located in Hubei Province of China.
The Wuhan Coronavirus was named Severe acute respiratory syndrome coronavirus 2 (SARS-CoV-2). The Wuhan Coronavirus causes an illness or a disease known as COVID-19. Now COVID-19 is a highly infectious respiratory condition caused by Wuhan Coronavirus. This Wuhan novel coronavirus measures 400 – 500 micrometres.

The prefix and suffixes like Wuhan and -19 help different the present virus from other coronaviruses.

The COVID-19 caused by Wuhan Coronavirus is highly contagious. It has created a global pandemic and is characterized by fever and other respiratory symptoms.

As of 3rd March 2020, the Wuhan coronavirus had already spread throughout the regions of China, Europe, United States and the Middle East. As of March 7th 2020, the virus can be found in all continents except Antarctica, which is mostly inhabitable.

From the subsequent sections and chapters of this book, you will get to know how to differentiate the symptoms, effects, and other characteristics of this novel Coronavirus.

Symptoms of Coronavirus:

According to WHO and UNICEF; the symptoms of Coronavirus (COVID-19) are these. They include:

Fever (Affects 98% of the infected)

Cough (affects 76% of the infected)

Shortness of breath (affects 55% of the infected)

Diarrhea (Affects 3%)

Sore throat (Affects 0% of the infected)

Ventilator support (9.8% of the infected people will eventually need it)

Fatality rate as of March 10th 2020 is 3.5% with over 109, 711 confirmed cases of infection worldwide. The average age of the infected is 49 years.

The COVID-19 cause dangerous viral pneumonia and antibiotics may be of no use if the condition gets to a particular stage.

Other symptoms to consider include:

- The unknown incubation period,

- Unexplained Fever or Malaise,
- Difficult breathing even when doing routine tasks,

- Impaired Liver, Kidney, Brain, and Heart functions,

- Severe cough,

- Pneumonia,

- And a general feeling of weakness.

In severe cases, the patient will come down with pneumonia, breathing difficulties, organs failures, and the disease could be fatal in older adults with pre-existing conditions.

The symptoms of coronavirus are like symptoms found in other common diseases, but respiratory effects which don't recede is a pointer that could alert you to visit the hospital.
Prognosis is good if you go to the hospital earlier.

The Coronavirus trek to lower respiratory tract marks the severe phase of the disease.

Progression of COVID-19 goes from mild or moderate to severe. This can happen quickly.

The symptoms cause cough and sneezing, but this virus causes more than just a cough. It stays in the throat and nose, but danger occurs when the infection gets to the lungs of the infected person.
One in seven people infected with COVID-19 experience difficulty in breathing, accompanied by other serious complications.

Some 6% of the people become critical, and these patients suffer respiratory failure and failure of other vital systems of the body.

Sometimes, infected persons develop septic shock. This report of patients developing 'septic shock' was gotten from Joint WHO-China mission on Feb. 2020.

The progression of coronavirus version 2019 is so fast and can occur very quickly.

Over 10% of patients with mild or moderate symptoms quickly progress to severe phases, and over 15% of these people become critical.

Greatest Risk Factor:

Presently, being in Wuhan in Hubei province or being in other Chinese provinces is among the top risk factors. Also, being in countries like Italy, South Korea and other states with larger numbers of infected people poses a significant risk too.

Having direct contact with an infected person

Having contact with respiratory droplets from an infected person

The people at the highest risk are adults aged 60years and older.

Those aged 60 and older with pre-existing conditions like hypertension, diabetes and cardiovascular diseases.
Those aged 60 years and above are also more likely to die from the COVID-19 with those with the pre-existing condition having the highest risk and fatality rate.

The spread of Disease and Complications:

COVID-19 spread is not much different from what we see in severe influenza.

Everyone is at risk, but COVID-19 is mostly spread via virus-laden droplets. The droplets from an infected person's cough, breathe, or sneeze transmits this virus to another.

The infection starts from the nose, then down to the lower respiratory tract. Once the virus has gotten into the body, it invades the epithelial cells that protect and line the respiratory tract of humans.

If the spread is contained in the upper respiratory tract, the result becomes less severe because the prognosis is better in such a case.

If the virus treks and gets down to the lower windpipe regions like the peripheral branches of the reparatory tract and the lung tissue, then the situation becomes critical. When it gets to the lower branches, it triggers more severe phases of the disease, making prognosis less unlikely to be good. The most severe phase is because of the pneumonia-causing damage coupled with secondary damage caused by antigen-antibody reactions.

Usually, the body's immune system responds to the infection and these results in more damage to the already strained respiratory tract.

The body can repair some of the damaged parts of the lungs, and the white blood cells will attack and scavenge on the pathogens and also help heal the tissue. The white blood cells are always the first-responders, and if this goes well, you recover from the disease within a few days of infection.

In more serious cases, the body's ability to repair and heal itself becomes too cumbersome, and this leads to the destruction of both health and virus-infected cells.

If the infection is not contained at the upper respiratory tract, the body's immune may begin to destroy healthy cells, and there is almost no ability to keep stuff out of the lower respiratory tract. When this happens, the lungs become venerable to secondary bacterial infections and germs usually restricted to the nose and throats moves into the lungs. Antibiotic-resistant bacteria also move in to cause more damage.

Usually, when 50% of the lungs are developed with Fibrosis, it becomes too late because, at this point, a lot of damage has been done.

The secondary bacterial infections are the worst scenario because this threat kills critical respiratory tract stem cells which could have helped repair and rejuvenate the scarred tissues of the lungs.

Without the stem cells in tissues, one can't get physically, and the lungs can't be repaired too.

When the lungs are unable to heal within moments; vital organs get starved of oxygen. The vital organs like liver, brain, kidney and heart suffer from impairments due to lack of oxygen.
At this stage of infection, everything begins to fall in cascade, and at this point, the infected person begins to go downhill.

At this point, the person becomes critically irredeemable and will possibly not get back to normal again.

According to studies from WHO, etc., the tipping point or the severe spread occurs faster in older people.

Healthy younger people are also not free because some have succumbed to the disease even after receiving antiviral, antibiotics; oxygen and blood pump to an artificial lung.

From some of the unconfirmed studies, some people seem to be more genetically susceptible. The study postulates that the abundance of shaped protein receptors in the respiratory tract makes one more at risk of complications.

Most individuals who die from this disease have some kind of immunodeficiency or any other host factors that relate to underlying illnesses.

Although the virus could be fatal, getting diagnosis very early is very important to survival.

The spread of COVID-19 can happen very rapidly, and most people may reach a critical stage before even seeking medical care. Noticing any of the above symptoms should be a prerequisite to getting tested.

Death is caused by various complications but majorly due to lack of oxygen in vital organs like heart, kidney, liver and the brain. Invasive secondary infections, adverse antigen-antibody reactions, immunodeficiency, respiratory failure and deficiency of stem cells which effects repair cause one to enter the end-stages of this novel pandemic virus. The virus will kill the infected when multiple organ failures set in.

How it affects the body:

COVID-19 enters the body through the nose, throat or mouth. The virus moves down to the lungs and in the lungs causes serious scarring of the lungs tissue. The stem cells can naturally repair this damage within days but invasive bacterial infections attacks and kill off the stem cells.

Due to the lack of stem cells, the lungs become unable to heal from the damage. The inability of the lungs to supply oxygen to the liver, kidney, brain and heart caused organ failure in these vital organs of the body.

The infection also causes bad episodes of antigen-antibody reaction. In antigen-antibody adverse response, the body's immune system attacks and destroys the virus-infected cells of the body and also destroys the healthy cells of the body. This immune attack further destroys stem cells.

The lack of oxygen in vital body organs leads to severe complications, and the person is unable to live any longer.

The COVID-19 is not curtailed to the nose or throat; it attacks the susceptible part of the respiratory system (lungs). Death follows when the body can't take any of these any longer.

For those with pre-existing conditions like cardiovascular disease. Lack of oxygen to the cardiac tissues causes tissue death, cardiac arrest, and death.

It affects the body like a host of grenade and disrupts the typical physiological path of the respiratory system leading to organ failures and death.

Generally, precautions, preventions and early detection help keep the virus spread in check.

Preventions, Precautions and Us:

Since the outbreak of this virus, many precautions have been taken by various individuals and bodies.

To prevent getting infected; follow these simple tips:

1. Stay indoors as much as possible and avoid crowded places
2. Avoid contact with other people who show any signs of flu no matter how minimal
3. Call N.H.S. if you notice any abnormalities and also inform them of your recent travel area
4. Avoid the countries worse hit by the disease; some of these countries include China, Korea and Italy.
5. Be very cautious with cleanliness and hygiene.

Precautions include but not limited to:

Medical experts in Taiwan gave a method of self-testing whether you have the novel Coronavirus.

If you don't have chest pain, cough, stress or fever, you might still be at risk because the incubation period of Coronavirus is not yet fully known. To self-test yourself,

Be in a very clean environment, hold your breath for 10seconds and if you don't have any cough, chest pain, no discomfort, stress; that means the lungs have no fibrosis hence no infection. You are entirely risk-free when you try this once in a while. Be sure to visit the hospital if you notice discomfort, chest pain, stress and cough.

1. Manage, treat and handle underlying health issues like diabetes, hypertension, pneumonia, respiratory disease and any form of immunodeficiency.
2. Wash your hands frequently with soap and clean water. Wash at least 10 seconds and scrub the hands thoroughly.

3. Cover your mouth and nose when you sneeze or cough
4. Use your elbow and bend over when you sneeze or cough
5. Don't get close enough to get in contact with people's respiratory droplets
6. Follow the advice from W.H.O., UNICEF and other trusted health organizations.
7. Discard and avoid speculation and false information.
8. Discard properly and Throw away the tissues or any materials you cough with.
9. Stay away from things like ice cream and avoid cold weather.
10. Avoid eating fish, meat, eggs and other animal products that are not well boiled or half-cooked.
11. Take a bath as often as possible and don't get any close to people when it is not necessary.
12. Be careful with food products and foods you order outside the country or within the country. Some of them may be contaminated. The virus can survive 12hrs outside the human host.
13. The Coronavirus can survive in hard surfaces for up to 12 hours hence wash your hands as often as you get the chance.

For us, COVID-19 is a serious issue and has affected various aspects of our lives. The best we can do is helping ourselves by following the preventions, precautions and maintaining good personal hygiene.

The virus has spread throughout the continents; hence no place is 100% safe. It is wise to always maintain good health profile and desist from any form of self-treatment.
The medical experts have also given a precaution measure. Everyone should try to avoid drying of the throat and mouth. Try to drink some fluids (water) every 15minutes, even if it is as little as a sip.

The virus enters the mouth; if this happens, the water moves it down to the stomach, and the high stomach acids destroy it before it starts any spread in the body. Please note that this is a precautional measure for the non-infected persons and not a cure for the virus.

Treatment for COVID-19:

As of March 2020, there has been no medicine to prevent, treat or manage Coronavirus.

The medical procedures aim to keep the lungs from getting further bad, helping prevent organ failures through an artificial blood pump to the lungs and also managing the infections with antivirals, antibiotics and other medications.

For now, the best treatment for coronavirus 2019 strand is to stay safe and practise necessary hygiene measures as outlined by W.H.O., UNICEF and other health institutions.

Pregnancy and Coronavirus:

Till this day, No studies have shown if a mother can pass the illness to her fetus or what the impact might be. Pregnant mothers are advised to be extra careful and safe because their condition could make the sickness very fatal if infected.

Race and Coronavirus:

For now, no definite-confirmed studies have shown if some people are genetically susceptible to Coronavirus.

Taubenberger said: Some people may be more genetically susceptible due to the higher abundance of the distinctly shaped protein receptors in their respiratory epithelial cells. These cells are what the virus targets.

Although the disease spread in Africa and other temperate regions might have been perceived as lesser, this could be related to weather.

Influenza and other respiratory-infectious illness usually thrive well during the winters. Hot temperatures could naturally be unfavorable to COVID-19 spread and progression.

The research from Genetic analysis by Chinese scientist has said that people with L strain have more prevalence than people with S strain. 70% of the disease can be found in people with l strain though this study is only speculations as it has not been confirmed

The Question of 'FACE MASK:

Coronavirus measures around 400 – 500 micrometres. If you have any mask that can protect against such diameter, then, you are good to go, but this is very unlikely because such a mask can't allow you to breathe well either. Nose mask is needed for those with the infection because it helps reduce the rate of spread.

Since the outbreak, the nose mask has been used as the insignia of prevention and protection. This might not be the case. Nose mask is not harmful, but it offers little to no protective function.

Note that Nose mask doesn't prevent Coronavirus. If you are not infected with COVID-19, there is no need to wear a nose mask. Washing of hands with water and soap or washing it with alcohol-based hand wash is more important.

Staying away from an infected person, practicing safe hygiene, managing pre-existing condition is way more important than nose mask or any form of face mask.
If you are not infected with the virus, there is no reason to wear a nose mask. UNICEF has also published this information.

Wearing of a mask is not harmful either, but the washing of hands is more important.

General Timeline of the Coronavirus rapid spread:

As of March 6 2020, the global death toll from Coronavirus was 3, 700 according to reports from John Hopkins University Center for Systems Science and Engineering.

More than 100,000 people have been infected in more than 82 countries. The death toll has passed in 3500 in China alone where the disease originated. There are over 80 000 cases of confirmed infections.

After China, South Korea and Italy is another nation worst hit by the Coronavirus outbreak. It has recorded about 7, 593 cases each. More than 55, 000 people in China have recovered from this novel Coronavirus (COVID-19).

The virus is worst than influenza and SARS, and there has been no vaccine or treatment so far. Italy has confirmed 366 deaths and Iran reported 49 new fatalities from the illness.
France, the US, Thailand, Syria, Nepal, Pakistan, Iraq, Egypt, Indian, South Africa and Switzerland has all confirmed cases of COVID-19.

From January 2020, the US, France and Australia reported confirmed cases of the virus and the spread has continued till now.
The US has also recorded at least 12 deaths since March 8 2020.

All the continents except Antarctica have confirmed cases of COVID-19, and its spread is always extensive and rapid.
The latest countries to confirm new cases are Nigeria (1), Armenia (1) and Jordan (1). Other countries have cases ranging from (4) to thousands.

East Asia, Europe and the Middle East are the worst hit continents. Africa has the least number of people infected with the new virus.

Since the outbreak of the disease was first made public in December 2019, the spread has been rapid, widespread and unpredictable. China announced first death on January 11, 2020, and now the global death toll is over 4,000 as of March 12 2020.

Due to the spread, the death toll and susceptibility; the COVID-19 has merited a spot as a Global Pandemic and a disease of Global Public Health Emergency.

Global Public Health Emergency?

Global Public Health Emergency or Public Health Emergency of International Concern is when the World Health Organization makes a formal declaration of an "extraordinary event which is determined to constitute a public health risk to other States through the international spread of the disease". Such a condition also needs International cooperation, response and measures.

A disease of global public health concern is 'serious, sudden, unusual, unexpected and risky' and carries implications to national borders or may require an immediate response from international action.

The legal duty of every State is to respond to such disease with all measures and commitment.

SARS, Smallpox, Wild Type Poliomyelitis and New Human influenza are diseases that have been declared Global Public Health Emergency.

Radio nuclear materials, chemical agents and some biomechanical agents can also be declared Global Public Health Concern as this is not restricted to disease outbreaks alone.

In any case, any disease or condition that falls within this category calls for serious "call to action" and "last resort" measure.
Most epidemics don't qualify as PHEIC (Public Health Emergency of International Concern) and have not been declared as such. The Fukushima Nuclear Disaster in Japan wasn't proclaimed a PHEIC.

On January 2020, The WHO declared the outbreak of Wuhan Coronavirus or COVID-19 is a PHEIC. COVID-19 is a Global Public Health Emergency.

Infections and Deaths:

Globally, over 100, 000 people are infected with the disease and over 3, 800 people have died from the COVID-19 outbreak (2020, March 8.)

The infections are more in Wuhan, Hubei and all provinces in China. After China, Italy and South Korea are the worst States hit by this deadly outbreak, and more than 366 people have died in Italy as of March 8, 2020.

The States with the least infection are Nigeria, Armenia and Jordan. The continent of Antarctica has no known COVID-19 disease.

Some conspiracy Theories surrounding COVID-19

After the sudden outbreak of this novel strand coronavirus. Many theories started affecting us even more than the virus itself.

The most basic is that the origin of the virus, Wuhan, home of the Wuhan Institute of virology is suspicious.

From this institute, some sources claimed that an experiment went wrong, and an accidental lab activity brought this virus into the world.

Some other theories suggest that the virus was released on purpose. The question of who, why, and what was precisely being targeted keeps being shroud in mystery.

There are some more lucid explanations, but we still can't ignore the possibility of the virus being engineered. Rumors of lab escape have had a concocted history of some kind of racism, amnesia and caricatured villain attached to it.

Other theories suggest that it was from the United States of America. The US and China have been going through a series of trade and economic wars.

The later and the former have been doing this for decades, but Trump's administration has made the relation a bit fragile.

The theories suggesting that this is a bioweapon have been strongly refuted, and the US has no justification for doing such a thing. Countries engage in brawls all the time, and the City of Wuhan have no part to play in the power struggle at least no significant impact to play.
Yes, such things always happen when such global emergencies emerge. Even during the SARS, Ebola and Polio outbreak, some people suspected other countries or their opponents.

We often have under-budgeted public health affair even in the most developed countries like the USA. Funds meant for public health programs have been defunded almost whenever there are no threats.

Labor laws, Health care reforms and other institutions may often look the other way when certain issues don't pose an immediate danger.

More than 15years after the last SARS outbreak, the world has not put in enough work to handle this global emergency.

It's easy to say it was attacked on China, but this disease has also started ravaging other countries around the world.
The COVID-19 has similarities with SARS, and its form appears to have mutated and modified a lot. This is what viruses do in other to avert easy eliminations.

Things don't always appear as we hear it. These theories are yet to present any solid proof. The only reliable assurance is the fact that this virus emerged from Wuhan's illegal bushmeat market.

After the SARS break 15years ago, the world should have developed a better vaccine, a cause and a program of elimination.

Since 2002, we have been venerable to this outbreak, and it has eventually happened. The COVID-19 is likely a product of neglect from us because we refused to take cues from the last SARS outbreaks.

The best we can do is to do our possible best to eliminate, curtail and manage the damage caused by this disease.
The conspiracy theories shouldn't affect us more than the virus because most of these theories are mere speculations with no fact or evidence.

After overcoming this virus; I hope the health system and all countries pay more attention to public health, and more funds should be allocated to health matters because health is paramount.

Coronavirus and Business:

Most disease outbreaks have little impact on global business. China is the most populated country on earth with supply chains and a hub for many productions and deliveries.

The outbreak of Coronavirus has caused serious upends in business and production.

As of Feb 28, 2020; The New York Times has some reports on the impact of this spreading virus.

The COVID-19 outbreak has rattled the flourishing global economy, disrupted supply chains, closing off access and flow of lucrative consumer market.

The outbreak has affected almost all sectors ranging from food, fashion, entertainment down to automobiles and technology.

It has also affected the service section as the panic has caused more people to withdraw from work. The shopping areas of major Chinese cities like Beijing, hundreds of shops have remained closed due to fear and safety.

The government has called on people to get back to work, but hundreds of stores still remain under lock and keys even in the capital cities.

The sports industry has also taken a hit as significant sports activities that involve top-coronavirus-hit countries have been suspended until further notice.
Even One month into the crisis, their economic crisis is yet to calm down, and more people are getting infected by the day.

It is expected that much of China should have opened by now, but the reverse is the case as the counties are empty. The countries industries are quiet, factories closed, the street empty and legions of workers have suggested months or weeks of break.

These impacts could take months before the economy could get back to normal again.
For decades, companies like Nike, Disney, Hyundai and McDonald's rely on China's capable and efficient factories and consumers.

This virus has forced many people to remain in their country and no movement to places like China and other high endemic areas.

Some countries obtain almost everything, including cars, video-games, and other supply chains from China and this crisis has rippled these supplies making it complicated.
The full financial impact of this virus is still too early to assess, but from all indications; it will be a big blow to the global economy.

Unarguably, China is taking the worst hit, and other countries like Italy are also following in this unfavorable trouble.

In the Film industry, Company like Imax of Canada has been forced to postpone the release of five films which was supposed to be showcased in China during the Lunar New Year Holiday.

In Japan, the Nintendo has delayed its video games supply, and on Feb 12 to 18 China asked over 41 casinos to close for 2weeks because of the high risk of being in such a crowded place.

Tim Cook, the CEO of Apple, has said that the supplies will be disrupted because its stores in China had dropped following the outbreak of the virus.

Apple has huge sales in China, and it assembles most of its products in China. Till now, Tim Cook says most of the stores would be closed in China and traffic has also fallen off the grid.

In Spain, the tech industries are putting restriction measures in place. People from Wuhan or Hubei province are restricted from entering the country, and any visitors from this area are not welcomed at this moment.

In China, many auto plants have shut down, and these factories include but not limited to Nissan, Telsa and Ford Motors.

In Japan, the plant in Kyushu has shut down due to reduced supplies from China. This company will resume production soon.

In Europe, there have been impacts. The travel sector has been seriously restricted for fear of imported virus spread.

Weeks and after weeks, airlines keep canceling flights to China and analyst expects this impact to be reduced, but the situation is getting better as expected.

The Cruise industry is not left out in this dilemma as Royal Caribbean Cruise has been barred for all people holding Chinese, Macau and Hong Kong passports. Those bearing these countries' passports are temporarily restricted from boarding its ships until further notice.

The Food industry is even more hit in China. Over 3500 restaurants have closed in China. Experts believe the profits would be reasonably small, but the virus has not been contained till now.

The Starbucks, Yum Brands and other food industries have also closed down. Half of Nike's stores in China have remained closed since February.

These damages are also carefully tripping toward other business sectors. Businessmen and women can't travel freely again due to the fear of infection, and some airlines have places they chose not to go.

The States around the world has also enacted restrictions to safeguard their country with many airports doing stop and examine in the airports.

The panic is even more than the real effects in business. The people have refused to go to work in certain areas.
The United States of America is also not left out in this ranging virus. As of Mar 10, many industries have noticed a significant drop in profits and companies like Apple has also reported a significant reduction.

The US and China are important trade partners and rivals, and this virus has also taken a toll, although the effect can't be ascertained until later during the month.

Travel and evacuations ensured after the outbreak, and many economic, strategic places in China have remained empty since then. This directly affects the US and some of its production industries who need the enormous population of China to sale more goods and services.

The Arab world has also reported impacts, and hike in deaths and infections have been reported too. The rate of free movement has decreased a bit because business people are now afraid of getting in contact with more people during this time of virus spread.

The Coronavirus has significantly affected the global supply chain by Mid-March. It has disrupted manufacturing operations, and its effects keep increase on a global scale. The worst is yet to come, but the present situation is also not looking good in any way.

Plants in the US and Europe have also been temporarily shut down. The companies worst affected are those who depend heavily on Chinese materials and parts.

For the past few months, these companies have fallen into unexpected disadvantages, and they are expected to be depressed for months or years as the case may be.

In the SARS outbreak of 2002 – 2003; the global economy suffered a significant blow. Now, China is a relatively important nation in a worldwide economic ecosystem, and this country has increased its economy at a tremendous rate for the past 18years.

In the global scale, China alone represents about 16% of the world GDP, and there is almost a four-fold increase by each passing year.
The pressure, expenses and current government efforts have quarantined almost one half of its population.

If I may say, the effect of COVID-19 will be more impactful than the SARS of 2002. The relatively important position of China in global business gives a clue on the devastating impact this virus poses on us.

African countries which mostly depend on China's supplies, especially on auto and techs have also started to feel the heat.
Every part of the world will feel the heat because plants in S Korea, US, Europe and other parts of the world have taken some moments of break and this means less productivity and more demand because people have been dodging to go to work now.

The challenge is even more in high-tech industries; even Apple reported that its quarterly earnings were lowered than previously expected.

Bridal gowns and other clothing materials sold all over the world are also affected.

The world should be ready for some major effects, especially on the manufacturing sector across the globe.

Within weeks, months and more of the outbreak, there would be heat on almost all economies. We can only hope that a cure is found as fast as possible, and we hope this doesn't cause any global recession. Countries that depend on China for supply and services will surely have a lot to battle within the coming months.

2-months to its spread; Coronavirus has caused a significant effect in business. You wouldn't expect less from a country that houses more than 1.4Billion people.
This population is equivalent to 18.47% of the total world population, and yes, the effect will surely be felt. It has already started, but we hope it can be curtailed to a considerable level.

Studies from IBM, Goldman Sachs, PwC and others have outlined the serious global threat to the global workplace. Workers are advised to work from home when possible, and you can imagine the effect of this on the long-run.

The US markets have also been plunging sharply since mid-Feb, 2020. Restrictions, drop in production, the shutdown of plants, cancelled trips, working from home, panic and expenses surely have effects on the economy. The strategic importance of China, the widespread of the disease, its mode of transmission and the fear it creates are the major factors affecting business, production, and global economy.

What's next?

Now that this virus has already spread and is causing devastating damage across the globe, what is the hope of the human race?

The plague has already started; we now need to count our losses and further strive to live just as we have always done in the past.

Experts and great thinkers have weighed up the worst and best-case scenarios—the WHO has already proclaimed it a global health emergency which is a step towards the right direction.

For now, these are some of the answers that answer the question of our curiosities; 'what next'?

Experts in China have postulated that this epidemic has shown rapid spread and devastation effects on both the economy and health.

In China, experts have predicted that the Coronavirus could infect over 30million people in the region of Wuhan if a cure is found within months.

They believe the virus has gone out of hand and it has also spread too far. Virologist Ian Mackay said that the virus spread too far, too quickly and has gone far more than expected.

In the best-case scenario, fewer people may be infected, but that seems not to be the case as hundreds are getting infected daily.

Other experts like Ben Cowling of Hong Kong University said; it's too early to determine whether quarantine, use of face masks and other measures can curtail this virus. The incubation period, which is tentatively 14days is longer than most control measures can contain; hence this virus is a hard one to manage.

The virus can become endemic if it circulates continuously in communities and many countries. The Chickenpox, Influenza and some other virus have become endemic in certain countries, and the outbreaks are only being controlled with vaccinations.

If Coronavirus is not contained; then, there is a good chance, it will become endemic, and this will be a challenging situation in the long run.

When the virus spreads without showing symptoms, it will be more challenging to control, and this will likely make the virus to be endemic, and several infected people don't display symptoms. Most infections show some subtle symptoms, while others have unnoticeable symptoms.

If the studies conclude that this virus can be asymptomatic, then the virus is going to stay a long time; possibly forever.

During the SARS outbreak in 2002-03, people were sick enough to need hospital care, and that was why SARS was easier to contain.

If the control measures turn out to be effective, then the virus could be eradicated from circulation before it infects more healthy individuals. Most people also argue if the virus will likely change. Medical Scientists and experts worry that as the disease keeps spreading, it could mutate and turn into something more serious. It could spread more efficiently and start causing young people to die if the virus undergoes changes.

For now, it is currently fatal for older people with conditions like diabetes, heart disease and cancer.

Some experts say that its mutations won't make it more virulent and this doesn't mean it will cause more serious diseases.

Most mutations are also detrimental to most viruses. The SARS of 2002 had mutations, and this reduced its virulence.
People also worry that the virus could kill more people than SARS. Yes, as of March 10th, the virus has already taken out more than 111, 000 people. It has shown a death rate of 3.7% lower than SARS which had a fatality rate of 10%.

Currently, there are no effective drugs against this novel virus. The H.I.V. drugs thought to target its proteins has been under study by scientists, but there has been no head-way so far on that.

For death rate reduction, putting people on ventilators and drips will help them get more oxygen and water, which is important as the immune system fights it.

If the virus spreads to low-income States in Africa and Asia; these States would struggle to contain with the demands of this virus and experts worry that this could lead to more deaths in such region.
In its declaration, the WHO's director-general said that the major concern is that this outbreak could spread to nations with fragile health systems. So far, it has even surpassed that ability and has infected first world countries with excellent health systems.

The coronavirus has a fatality rate of 3.7% lower than SARS, but yet it's still high for an infectious disease. The 1918 influenza outbreak, known as the Spanish Flu infected around half a billion people at the time.

This population was 1/3rd of the world's population then, and it killed 2.5% of those it infected. Most estimates say that as much as 50million people died from the Spanish Flu of 1918.

Although there is a great dread due to the statistics, many experts believe the novel COVID-19 won't be that apocalyptic because it isn't killing healthy young people.

Some Sportsmen, people in business, top politicians and citizens have tested positive to the disease. This disease doesn't select a social class. Its definite mode of spread has not been determined, as well.

The Coronavirus outbreak has left the world in awe. All measures to contain the disease have not been so effective, but these measures have at least reduced spread to a considerable level.

We hope that scientists and world experts find a cure as fast as possible. Now our fate lies in the hands of wonderful brains of these scientists and technologists.

CHAPTER EIGHT:

THE IMPACT OF CORONAVIRUS ON MENTAL HEALTH.

The pandemic and its impact on the community and in particular on the health of the population require comprehensive and integrated measures. Prioritizing, in this context, health over other analysis variables is an ethical duty that has achieved the general consensus of the different sectors. In any case, when defining the scope of this prioritization, sanitary measures have focused almost exclusively on reducing the increase in infections, the case curve being the only one visible. It is essential to broaden the perspective and understand the impact of the pandemic on the psychosocial health of the population and the consequences on their mental health .

A recent systematic review of the Lancet shows results compatible with negative psychological effects, the increase in stressors, the greater probability of lasting post-quarantine effects and the direct relationship between quarantine duration and impact on the population's mental health.

This probable situation should encourage the taking of measures to increase the approach to these problems. On the one hand, recommendations and actions have been outlined and are being implemented in the prevention, tracking and treatment of Covid-19 cases, but this is not the case with regard to mental health. In turn, when monitoring cases of people infected with Covid-19, the curve that flattened out in the first instance is then expected to begin to decline. On the other hand, regarding mental health, even after the decrease in the number of those infected with the new coronavirus, psychosocial problems may continue to emerge due to the consequences of isolation and social distancing.

On the other hand, regarding the detected cases of Covid-19, most of them require a brief treatment in terms of time, 14 days on average, and light care. Only a small percentage requires hospitalization and, to a lesser extent, treatment in intensive care units. Instead, the course and treatment of diagnosed mental health problems are mostly longer; therefore, they require a greater sustainability of the actions of the health systems over time.

What actions, then, should health systems take to correctly address the increase in mental health problems in these times? As the writer of this book with vivid research done on this particular topic, I propose an analysis based on three population groups. The first group is that of the general population without Covid-19 or mental illness caused by the pandemic. The second, the population with Covid-19 or with some unrecognized mental health problem, and therefore without response from the health system. The third group, those who have Covid-19 or a mental health problem that have been detected and are on treatment.

Regarding the first group, preventive actions are being developed. For the Covid-19, recommendations for hygiene measures and preventive and mandatory social distancing are made. They are clear and massive measures. Regarding mental health, self-care recommendations are made in a disparate way to minimize the negative impact of isolation. In both cases, the actions are aimed at maintaining and increasing the size of this group, avoiding contagions and mental illnesses.

Regarding the second group, the measures are aimed at reducing their magnitude, that is, increasing the amount of case detection, but in a very uneven way. Tracking measures are implemented for Covid-19, such as socialization of alarm guidelines, mobile self-assessment applications, temperature measurements and testing. In mental health, without trying to draw a parallel on two situations that are not completely assimilable, we are faced with a deficit of interventions. This generates a significant accessibility gap, which will undoubtedly increase the existing gap considerably if measures are not planned to address it. It is not a matter of "tracing psychopathologies in the population" or of pathologizing or medicalizing ailments typical of everyday life today crossed by the crisis,

In the third group, as well as guaranteeing the treatment of people with Covid-19, it is important that there is also availability of timely treatment of mental health problems, both remotely and by technological means such as face-to-face, in cases where it was essential due to the problem or access difficulties.

Are health systems ready to provide these mental health responses for all three population groups? The measures of health promotion and primary prevention in mental health, through recommendations, can and should be implemented from the community areas of the health networks, with a strong participation of the first level of care. The same is true for detecting and addressing most mental health problems, which can be solved at that level, just as the treatment of most Covid-19 cases: in mental health, only a small Percentage requires a specialized approach at the second level of care, interventions on duty in hospitals, psychiatric care, medication, and even brief hospitalizations.

This updates the debate regarding the role of the first level of care. It is necessary to strengthen the interdisciplinary territorial health teams, which have a lot to do in this context. It is the same problem as always, reducing the gap, increasing accessibility and even more effective coverage, and then continuity of care. Only in this way will we have comprehensive health interventions in the context of the pandemic. There is not a single curve. To make both visible is to understand that there is no health without mental health.

The Pandemic Takes A Psychological Toll

In these days when there is so much talk about the economic footprint that the coronavirus crisis will leave, it is also important to deal with the psychological footprint that it may have produced in us and that could affect us for the next few weeks, maybe even months. If at the beginning of the confinement, according to a survey carried out by EAE Business

School, the emotions of the Spanish were quite positive - only 5% said they were very afraid, 17.5% felt really sad and 73% felt safe. Now is the time to check how the time that has passed has fostered feelings of fear, sadness or insecurity.

Quarantine is often associated with a negative psychological effect, something that is not surprising during the period of isolation. However, there is evidence that this effect can still be detected months or years later. "

How can we prepare ourselves to emotionally overcome the mark that the experience lived over the last few weeks has left on us?

Watch for the signs. Relief at seeing the situation improve may be accompanied by an emotional slump. In the traumatic situation we endure, we pull ... but, when we begin to see the exit, it is frequent that we allow ourselves to fall. "It is then when we must attend to symptoms such as stress, anxiety, low mood; they can be an indicator of post-traumatic stress .

What can we do. Reacting as if nothing had happened can make problems appear later, so now it is convenient to try to do an introspection exercise, look inside ourselves and try to identify our emotions so that, from there, we can accept them. It is useful to verbalize the thoughts, that is, put them into words: we can do it in writing, if we feel more comfortable, or by sharing them with others.

Get rest. After months of alertness and changing time routines, it is not easy to let down your guard. One of the signs of post-traumatic stress is difficulty falling asleep. But it is a vicious circle: if we have anxiety, we don't sleep well, and if we don't sleep well, anxiety increases us (one of the functions of rest is to reduce this anxiety). According to a study by the Global Sleep Observatory, "insomnia affects between 20 and 30% of the population. And one of the main reasons for not sleeping well are the worries that arise during the night and the excessive mental activity: 'thinking too much'. This prevents the body from leaving the state of alert and makes it difficult to fall asleep.

Although it costs us, we must try not to alter the sleep-wake rhythm. For this, we will try to go to bed and get up at the usual time. Relaxation exercises can help us free the mind from obsessive thoughts, but a useful technique when we are overwhelmed by worries is to quote and review our problems. It is about writing down on paper everything that worries us and that we cannot solve at this time, understanding what is up to me. It is very important to define it, to put energy exclusively into what we can solve.

Handle grief

If the death of a loved one is always difficult, it is even more difficult not to have been able to say goodbye to it to prevent contagion. Feelings of guilt may arise for not telling you what we felt, what we loved, as well as feelings of helplessness and frustration.

What can we do. Once the situation has passed, it may be time to celebrate an act or a ceremony to remember that person who is no longer there, and ask our family and friends to join us. Although postponed in time, it is an opportunity to overcome the duel among all.

Other losses. Even if we have not lost a loved one, there are other duels that we will have to go through. We have all lost something in this crisis: it may be employment, but also the resignation of some project –vital or professional–, the frustration of having to start from scratch or the emptiness that has left us having spent weeks without being able to be with people those we want and need.

What can we do. In this type of traumatic situation, it is completely normal to feel sad, frustrated and angry. Each of us will need an adaptation time to integrate the trauma in his life and to be able to build from it. The next phase is to harness the energy and see how we can, when the situation is right, reconvert ourselves. You have to accept and accept the new situation and dedicate energy to new projects.

Combat mistrust. The word resentment refers to "feeling again." Therefore, if we let ourselves be carried away by this resentment we revive the rancor: to the politicians, the authorities, the invading bug, toxic news, mismanagement and reality. All of this leads to mistrust. Moving in suspicion and suspicion increases uncertainty and does not allow us to move forward. As long as we stay there, we will not regain confidence.

What can we do. It is one thing to be mindful and critical and quite another to move suspiciously and apprehensively. We may feel deceived, but it is also important to identify what has been done well, and from the heart. "Working from forgiveness is liberating. It does not have to do with faith, but with not looking for the bad intentions of others. A good exercise is to exchange a grudge for gratitude. From farmers to stockers, from toilets to transporters, from cleaners to volunteers.

..With the little ones:

They have been with us for several weeks, seeing us at home at all times, and now we cannot disappear overnight. The separation must be gradual, and the new situation must be explained to them in words they can understand.

If our work has traditionally been very demanding and has left us little time for our children, now is the time to understand the meaning of the word 'reconciliation'.

Now that we have had the opportunity to play more with them, spend more time with them, make crafts or make up stories, let's try to keep these games and moments of intimacy within our routines.

You have to accept that it is going to take a lot of effort to rejoin your daily life. Just as after the holidays they need an adaptation period, now they will also need our patience.

Coping with fear

"Fear is a functional emotion that helps us face situations in which we are in danger. Fear has been useful to us , to understand that we had an enemy (the virus) and protect ourselves from it, as well as to identify the heroes who have helped us.

However, in the past few weeks we have become more vulnerable. We have realized that we may be at risk, and that perception has also been lived by our children. The 2013 study from Post-Traumatic Stress Disorder in Parents and Children after Health-Related Disasters from the University of Cambridge reveals that children who experienced quarantine had four times more post-traumatic stress than those who did not.

Another study, this one on the psychological impact of the SARS quarantine experience, concludes that 54% of people who had been quarantined avoided people who coughed or sneezed, 26% avoided closed places, and 21% He avoided all public space in the weeks after the quarantine period. On the other hand, special care must be taken with older people, who will probably have felt with greater intensity the fear of dying from the infection; That fear has made them face their vulnerability, especially because of the repeated messages that they are the collective at risk.

What can we do. Once the crisis is over, our brain is going to look for strategies to make that fear adaptive, transitory. It will look for arguments and explanations to calm down. We will go in search of the rational. In children it will be easier, they have a greater capacity for adaptation, but our attitude will be decisive in making them overcome their fears: we must transmit calm and offer them security. Let us try not to talk about our fears and anxieties in their presence: although it seems that they are not finding out, they have a great capacity to perceive emotions. It is also important to help them express how they feel, to listen to them and not to downplay their emotions. In the elderly, the best way will be that of affection and that of offering them new illusions (a family getaway,

Ask for professional help? Like fear, sadness or anger, they are functional emotions that may have arisen in a crisis like the one in Covid-19. Sadness makes us reflective and helps us to value life; Anger or anger also appear because on many occasions we need the relief of not understanding, all emotions have a function and predispose us to survival. The problem arises when they are of such intensity that they paralyze us and limit us in any day-to-day function.

General apathy may be a sign that we need professional help. When the introspection is not reflective, but of enclosure, when we only want to be with ourselves and from disruptive feelings (loneliness, abandonment, frustration), when we enter a whirlwind of negative emotions in which we have no tools to find a breath, a consolation. The GP can guide us on this path, but if we feel unable to find a professional, we can entrust ourselves to our closest people to help us find resources with which to improve our emotional situation.

People with disorders. Among the most vulnerable we find patients with depression. To his negative vision of life is added the set of unpleasant and alarming events that have unfolded.

If we have someone in our environment in these circumstances, it is very important that they feel protected. It is essential that they continue trying to maintain meal and rest schedules, since changes in chronobiological rhythms are negative for mental illness. They should also have a fixed routine, a schedule that includes work or domestic tasks, as well as leisure activities and contact with loved ones.

..With teenagers:

Although the relationship with them is not always easy, in the confinement we will have incorporated new routines: eating together, watching series, learning to bake a cake ... The objective is to try to keep these new spaces of union open, that they do not disappear.

We can help them appreciate the positive aspects that this experience has had: family union and participation in household chores, increased responsibilities and control of emotions.

It is also time to tell them that we have appreciated how they have been able to work on responsibility when studying from home, and teach them to value the figure of the teacher.

Try to avoid the 'hedonistic adaptation': that the joy of going out again and starting to recover the life of before does not fade in a matter of days. The objective is that they learn - and for this we must set an example - to appreciate and value the small pleasures of life.

In society: back to routine?

During the isolation we have been stocked with the basic products: food, hygiene, cleaning ..., but away from everything that is not necessary. A paradoxical situation, since, in situations of emotional stress, shopping can be an escape route that was not possible during this crisis. This can provoke in us a certain desire for revenge, a purchase to forget, because, "we are going to want to activate centers of pleasure, of enjoyment. It's easy to think that we need a reward after such a long time of effort. "

According to her, this will be especially seen in those who have not been affected from the economic point of view; they will consume, sometimes in an excessive way. It is a very emotional consumption. At the same time, it is also possible that, faced with the uncertainty of the economic future, we may be afraid of spending and become obsessed with saving. For example, we will not buy a car: according to the consultancy MSI, vehicle sales in Spain will drop almost 30% in 2020.

What can we do. If we have been financially penalized - from the closure of the company or the reduction of customers - we must maintain an adaptive attitude. It is about understanding that this period will be temporary and will allow us to develop competencies that we need, such as flexibility or adaptation to change. It may be time to reflect on responsible consumption and ask ourselves that, just as we have lived with very few things during isolation, we can continue like this for a while longer. This crisis can help us to discern the superfluous of the necessary.

Relate to others. At the beginning of the quarantine, we often told ourselves how much we were going to kiss and hug each other when the isolation ended. Over time, we understood that there would be a zero day in which everything would be the same as before. We have the example of what happened in China: several weeks after returning to work, the alert continues and with it new behaviors, such as the social distance of two meters - even when it is no longer compulsory -, the omnipresent masks and mistrust.

What can we do. Know how to wait. A period of adaptation, of acclimatization, is inevitable, and we will have to accept that, for some time, we will continue to feel apprehension at physical contact. But we can take advantage of another aspect of our relationship with others: we have all experienced examples of solidarity, such as altruistic help towards the elderly by the youngest, concern about the state of health of acquaintances with whom we had lost contact ... These new ways of meeting again can be as satisfying as a hug.

Interact daily again. For once, returning to work may represent the antithesis of the famous post-vacation syndrome. Just as the youngest can find enjoyment when they return to school or institute, when they meet up with classmates, we adults can also experience feelings of hope in the office, the office or the workshop. But, once again, it will not be the same for everyone: those who have a bad work environment and have enjoyed this period of teleworking - or even may now have a greater impact than the post-vacation syndrome.

CONCLUSION

Even though it may be hard for us to think positive, yet, we should always try to stay positive, with this we will win over any negative situations. It is to be expected that many things will have changed in the whole world, both in structures, living, economy, psychology and so on. Yet It is time to focus on the positive aspects of our working our life and what goes with it: camaraderie, human values, relationships with others, and maintaining a good and health living both before, during and after a pandemic. It is high time we stand tall, watchful and careful, and as well be courageous to face any world challenge that might befall every inhabitants.

www.ingramcontent.com/pod-product-compliance
Lightning Source LLC
Chambersburg PA
CBHW051437140726
47987CB00006B/2414